Photography by **Danielle Menashe Gindi**
Edited by **Lorraine Sherr**
Design by **OffWhite Design**

# DARE TO BE DIFFERENT

## VOLUME 2

### Turning up the heat

# WELCOME BACK!

I hope you enjoy my new book, *Dare to be Different*: *Turning up the heat*.

Entertaining through food is a great way for us to bond and bring families and friends closer together. The dinner table is a forum for us to communicate with those closest to us.

My home cooked meals are casual and delicious. I always start with the finest ingredients and a well-stocked pantry; allowing me to create with ease. When I'm having family or friends my goal is to organize early and enjoy their company.

Many of my recipes I make up as I experiment in the kitchen. But I also love dining in great restaurants and trying different foods then coming home and concocting recipes that add a twist to the taste. Cooking should be fun and easy. I wanted to create a collection of easy-to-follow, delicious dishes, simplifying the process and "turning up the heat" in a way that makes cooking fun.

About a year ago, I began introducing a hint of cayenne pepper, jalapeño, red pepper flakes and chili peppers and instantly fell in love with the new dimension it brings to the dishes. If you have never cooked with spice before, gauge my recipes. You can always begin with a lesser amount of spice and as you become accustomed to it, work your way up, adding a small bit at a time.

I find that through cooking we can put our hearts into our dishes and the results are astounding. This has always been my goal, to express myself through cooking and create a style that raises the bar in an easy and fun way. That is how I approached this collection and my "dare to be different" style.

Putting together this book enabled me to continue to enjoy the passion of cooking and continue to "dare to be different." I sincerely hope you enjoy this collection as much as I enjoyed bringing it to life.

I would like to take this opportunity to give special recognition to my partner in this project, Lorraine Sherr. Her unwavering dedication, loyalty, inspiration and creativity enabled us to produce our second edition of *Dare to be Different*.

Lorraine, you are so special to me. Your total support and love are the driving force behind this cookbook. Your passion, advice, ideas and never-ending time spent – no matter the situation – are what have produced a very special blend of recipes filled with character and personality. You are the continuous motivation behind this project and with whom I will share a special relationship and bond forever.

Lets always "dare to be different."

Love always – Robin

# THANK YOU!

**Thank you to Josh White and Adi Bereshit-Elias of OffWhite Design** for your creativity in putting together *Dare to be Different, Volume 2*. Your artistic vision and direction helped us to shape the flavor of *Turning Up The Heat*.

**A special thank you to my photographer, Danielle Gindi.** You captured the essence of my dishes and exceeded all of my expectations. Your passion for photography and easy-going manner make you terrific at what you do. Thanks for your patience, dedication and love!

**To my #1 fan and loving husband, Marvin:** Thanks for your help and encouragement; for never letting me give up and for being my best friend and #1 taste-tester. Thanks for putting up with my "recipe talk" no matter what time of day or night. If not for you *Dare to be Different* would be just a dream. I love you!

**Thank you to my daughters Sally, Lorraine, Allyson and Jennifer** and to my son-in-laws, **Robert, Jack and Solomon,** for your support, advice and suggestions. I always look forward to our Friday night dinners and Sunday barbeques when I get to experiment for you and your families. These weekly dinners unify us and keep us so close. Thank you for taste-testing all my concoctions: the good and the not-so-good! I love you all!

To my mom, Lorraine Gindi, who teaches me by example how to lead a life full of love and energy; how to do anything I aspire to with my fullest capability and how to let my passion for what I do reflect in my work. Mom, there is nothing that hinders your drive for life and accomplishment.

My appreciation goes out to my mother-in-law, Sally Jemal, for instilling in me the value of family. From the first years of my marriage, always modeling hospitality and how to lead an open home. You taught me how to navigate and create in the kitchen with much grace and ease!

Thanks to...
All my sisters, nieces and nephews for your drive-by taste testings and for your honest criticisms of my dishes. For experimenting in your own kitchens and for tweaking many of my recipes.

Elliot Chrem, for helping style many of our dishes and for enabling our photoshoots to run as smoothly and efficiently as possible. You are extremely talented and your love for what you do is evident in your food's presentation!

My sister-in-law, Paulette Jemal for taking the time out of your busy schedule to look through and edit my recipes.

Short cut tips

Being that so many of my recipes call for a sautéed chopped onion, I like to saute a bunch of onions at the beginning of the week and store them in the refrigerator. The sautéed onions remain fresh for up to a week and it just makes a new recipe much easier to make.

 My general rule when cooking is that my skillet, pot, tray or roaster should never be overcrowded. Always allow ample space for your dish to be evenly cooked, nicely browned and crisped.

 When a recipe calls for white or red wine, I suggest to use a wine that's is suitable for drinking.

 If a recipe calls for an ingredient that you don't have, don't get discouraged; simply leave it out or substitute it for something else.

 Some of my recipes call for broth: either vegetable or chicken. Being that many types of broth are high in sodium and unnatural additives, I like to use Imagine™ Chicken Broth or any organic broth, as they are low in calories and a healthy alternative to your ordinary broth.

# TABLE OF CONTENTS

## SALADS & SOUPS

Arugula Salad with Roasted Carrots & Limes.................16
Burghul Salad with Wilted Spinach & Raspberry Vinaigrette...............19
Tofu Avocado Salad................................................20
Fennel & Baby Artichoke Salad....................................23
Fattoush Salad....................................................24
Raw Vegetable Salad..............................................27
Warm Brussel Sprout Salad with Homemade Croutons................28
Roasted Cauliflower, Kale & Chickpea Salad......................29
Asian Chicken Salad..............................................31
Jalapeño Chicken Soup............................................32
Miso Soup........................................................34
Shurba Soup......................................................35
Roasted Zucchini Soup............................................37
Tomato Bean Soup.................................................38
Lentil Spinach Soup..............................................39

## APPETIZERS

Chicken Lettuce Wraps with Peanut Sauce and Asian Slaw..........42
Chicken Sliders..................................................45
Lamb Sliders.....................................................45
Spinach Ricotta Wontons..........................................47
Meat Wontons.....................................................48
Cheese Filled Wontons with Pesto.................................51
Vegetable Wontons................................................52
Short Ribs on Sticks.............................................53
Mediterranean Stuffed Tomatoes with Quinoa......................55
Greek Portabella Pizzas..........................................56
Vegetable Portabella Pizzas......................................57
Crispy Rice......................................................58
Eggplant & Zucchini Chips with Tzatziki..........................60

## SIDES & VEGETABLES

Grilled Corn with Toasted Coconut ............... 65
Stuffed Artichokes .............................. 66
Balsamic Flavored French String Beans ........... 69
Spaghetti Squash with Vegetables ................ 70
Crispy Artichokes ............................... 73
Shakshuka ....................................... 74
Potato Galette .................................. 76
Eggplant Rollatini with Pesto ................... 77
Roasted Butternut Squash with
Wasabi Peas ..................................... 78
Toasted Okra .................................... 81
Spinach & White Beans ........................... 82
String Beans with Flanken ....................... 84

## PIZZAS

Grilling a Pizza Dough .......................... 88
Arugula Salad Pizza ............................. 90
Brussel Sprout Mozzarella Pizza ................. 93
Grilled Vegetable Pizza ......................... 94

## PASTAS & GRAINS

Crispy White Spaghetti .......................... 99
Black Rice with Fennel & Pomegranates .......... 100
Pasta with Fresh Cherry Tomato Sauce &
Melted Mozzarella .............................. 102
Quinoa with Roasted Mushrooms &
Truffle Oil .................................... 105
Soba Noodles with Tehina Sesame Sauce .......... 106
Crispy Rice Apricot with Chicken ............... 108
Pasta Bolonese ................................. 111

## FISH

Blackened Grouper with Mango Corn Salsa ........ 114
Panko Crusted Tuna with Spicy Mayo ............. 116
Grilled Salmon with Dill Sauce ................. 119
Sea Bass Lettuce Cups with Shredded Fillo ...... 121
Slow Roasted Halibut ........................... 122

## CHICKEN

Baby Chicken Over French String Beans .......... 126
Tamarind Chicken with
Roasted Fingerling Potatoes .................... 129
Eggplant Chicken Pie ........................... 130
Spinach Chicken Burgers ........................ 133
Roasted Herb-Spiced Cornish Hens ............... 134
Broiled Eggplant Chicken Wrap .................. 137

## MEAT

Tangy Meat Tacos ............................... 141
Balsamic Glazed Rack of Lamb with
Espresso Rub ................................... 142
Breaded Rack of Lamb with Dijon & Rosemary ..... 144
Minute Steak Split ............................. 145
Eggplant & Meatballs ........................... 147
Lamb Riblets ................................... 148
Lorraine Gindi's Rack of Veal with
a Lemon Wine Sauce ............................. 151
Meat-Stuffed Artichokes ........................ 152
Pepper Crusted Fillet Mignon ................... 154
Veal Scallopini with a Tomato Mushroom Sauce .. 156
Korean Short Ribs .............................. 159
French Cut Roast ............................... 160
Hashu (Meat & Rice Stuffing) ................... 162
Veal Pocket Neck with Peas and Hashu ........... 163
Japanese Vegetable Bowl ........................ 165

## CONDIMENTS

Preserved Lemons ............................... 171
Preserved Lemon Roasted Garlic
Caesar Dressing ................................ 173
Spicy Mayo ..................................... 175
Sweet Pesto .................................... 177
Lemony Pesto ................................... 177
Caramelized Onions ............................. 179
Oven Roasted Tomatoes .......................... 181
Dill Mustard Sauce ............................. 183

# SALADS & SOUPS

Arugula Salad with Roasted Carrots & Limes............................16

Burghul Salad with Wilted Spinach & Raspberry Vinaigrette......19

Tofu Avocado Salad......................................................................20

Fennel & Baby Artichoke Salad...................................................23

Fattoush Salad..............................................................................24

Raw Vegetable Salad....................................................................27

Warm Brussel Sprout Caesar Salad with Homemade Croutons.28

Spicy Kale Salad with Roasted Chickpeas & Cauliflower..........29

Asian Chicken Salad....................................................................31

Jalapeño Chicken Soup................................................................32

Miso Soup.....................................................................................34

Shurba Soup.................................................................................35

Roasted Zucchini Soup................................................................37

Tomato Bean Soup.......................................................................38

Lentil Spinach Soup.....................................................................39

# ARUGULA SALAD
## WITH ROASTED CARROTS & LIMES

### INGREDIENTS

#### Carrots
1 pound carrots, cut in ¼'s (in half horizontally, then in half vertically)
2 tablespoons olive oil
1 ½ tablespoons agave
½ teaspoon cayenne pepper
1 teaspoon chopped fresh rosemary
1 teaspoon cumin
Juice of 2 limes

#### Lime Dressing
¼ cup orange juice
Juice of 3 limes
3 tablespoons olive oil
1 teaspoon agave
⅛ teaspoon cayenne pepper

#### Salad
2 cups baby arugula
Shelled sunflower seeds
1 avocado, diced

1. **Prepare carrots:** Place carrots on a greased baking tray and toss with oil, agave, cayenne pepper, rosemary, cumin and lime juice. Roast uncovered at 425°F for 45 minutes, turning once or twice in between.

2. **Prepare dressing:** Whisk together dressing ingredients.

3. **Assemble salad:** On a bed of arugula, place roasted carrots and a sprinkle of sunflower seeds. Scatter diced avocados around the circumference of the platter, pour dressing over salad and serve.

# BURGHUL SALAD

## WITH WILTED SPINACH & RASPBERRY VINAIGRETTE

### INGREDIENTS

½ cup coarse burghul
½ Vidalia onion, chopped
olive oil
1 cup water
salt
12 ounces fresh baby spinach
¼ cup dried cherries (or cranberries)
¼ cup sliced almonds, toasted

### Raspberry Vinaigrette Dressing

1 cup fresh raspberries
¼ cup oil
3 tablespoons red wine vinegar
3 tablespoons agave
1 tablespoon mustard
Pinch of red pepper flakes
2 tablespoons water

1. In a pot, sautéee onion in olive oil until its edges begin to golden. Add water to pot and bring to a boil. Add burghul and salt and boil until all water is absorbed. Cover and transfer to oven at 350°F for 20 minutes. Remove from oven and fluff bulghur with a fork.

2. **Prepare dressing:** In a food processor, combine dressing ingredients together and blend well.

3. **Arrange salad:** While bulghur is still hot, transfer it to a mixing bowl and add spinach, dried cherries and toasted almonds.

   Add dressing and mix together nicely, enabling spinach to slightly wilt.

# TOFU AVOCADO SALAD

## INGREDIENTS

1-12 ounce container extra-firm tofu, drained and patted dry and cut into 8 small triangles

Sweet or Lemony Pesto
(see recipes page 177)

### Dressing

⅓ of an avocado
1 cup fresh basil
½ cup olive oil
2 tablespoons fresh lemon juice
1-2 cloves garlic
salt
pinch of red pepper flakes

2 avocados, sliced
cherry tomatoes, halved

1. **Prepare & grill tofu:** Brush pesto onto tofu. In a grill pan over the stove, grill tofu (in a small amount of oil) for about 2 minutes on each side, until lightly golden.

2. **Prepare dressing:** In a food processor, combine dressing ingredients and blend well.

3. **Arrange salad:** In a platter, combine sliced avocados, cherry tomatoes and grilled tofu. Drizzle dressing over salad and toss well.

\*\* Serve at room temperature.

# FENNEL & BABY ARTICHOKE SALAD

### INGREDIENTS

8 baby artichokes, cleaned and halved
bowl filled with water and lemon juice
olive oil
4 preserved lemons, cut in ¼'s
salt
pepper
pinch of red pepper flakes
2 fennel bulbs, sliced on a mandolin
1 grapefruit, sections divided
1 avocado, diced

#### Dressing

juice of 2 fresh lemons
¼ cup olive oil
1 teaspoon salt
½ teaspoon pepper
1 teaspoon chopped fresh parsley, plus more for garnish
2 teaspoons red wine vinegar

1. **Prepare artichokes:** Remove tough outer leaves. Cut artichoke in half and remove choke with a spoon. As you work, place cleaned artichokes in a bowl filled with water with lemon juice.

2. Remove artichokes from water and dry well. Over the stove, add oil to coat the bottom of a wide pan. Add to pan: artichokes, lemons, salt and pepper and sautéee 6-8 minutes.

3. **Prepare dressing:** Whisk together dressing ingredients.

4. **Assemble salad:** Arrange sliced fennel on a platter with grapefruit and diced avocado. Pour dressing over salad and toss well. Add sautéed artichokes on top and garnish with chopped parsley.

# FATTOUSH SALAD

## INGREDIENTS

### Pita Chips

3 pita bread pockets

olive oil cooking spray

Zaatar spice

### Zaatar Dressing

¼ cup extra virgin olive oil

¼ cup original olive oil

1 ½ tablespoons salt

juice of 3 lemons

1 clove garlic

3 tablespoons fresh parsley

1 teaspoon honey

¼ teaspoon cayenne pepper

3 tablespoons zaatar spice

¼ of an avocado

### Salad

2 hearts of romaine, thinly cut

4 radishes, cut into ⅛ th's

2 tomatoes, chopped

1 avocado, cubed

4 stalks of celery, chopped

3 Kirby cucumbers, chopped

2 fresh ears of corn, boiled for 8 minutes and remove corn from the cob

½ bunch fresh parsley, chopped (divided, reserving 3 tablespoons for dressing)

1 tablespoon chopped fresh mint

1. **Prepare pita chips:** Preheat oven to 400°F. Cut pitas into 8-12 bite-size pieces and split each piece in half to make thin chips. Arrange pitas in a single layer on a baking sheet. Spray pitas with olive oil cooking spray and sprinkle Zaatar evenly over pita bites. Bake for 8-10 minutes or until chips are golden brown and crispy.

\*\* Pita chips can be made up to a day in advance and stored in an air-tight container.

2. **Prepare Zaatar dressing:** In a food processor, combine dressing ingredients and blend well.

3. **Assemble salad:** In a large salad bowl, combine salad ingredients and pita chips. Pour dressing over salad and toss well.

# RAW VEGETABLE SALAD

### INGREDIENTS

10 radishes, sliced on a mandolin
20 sugar-snap peas, sliced thin lengthwise
1 avocado, cubed
1 mango, cubed
2 tablespoons chopped fresh basil

#### Dressing

1 tablespoon olive oil
2 tablespoons fresh lemon juice
2 tablespoons rice vinegar
1 teaspoon salt
½ teaspoon pepper
¼ teaspoon cayenne pepper
1 tablespoon agave

1. Combine radishes, sugar-snap peas, avocado, mango and basil in a large bowl.

2. **Prepare dressing**: Whisk together dressing ingredients.

3. Pour dressing over salad and toss to coat.

# WARM BRUSSEL SPROUT CAESAR SALAD
## WITH HOMEMADE CROUTONS

### INGREDIENTS

brussel sprouts, cut in ⅓'s lengthwise
olive oil
salt
pepper

#### Homemade Croutons
1 whole-wheat baguette
olive oil
salt
garlic powder
red pepper flakes
Parmesan cheese, grated

Preserved Lemon Roasted Garlic Caesar Dressing
(see recipe page 173)
Parmesan cheese, shaved

1. **Prepare brussel sprouts:** Arrange brussel sprouts on a baking tray and toss with olive oil, salt and pepper. Bake uncovered at 400°F for 40 minutes.

2. **Prepare croutons:** Cut the baguette into even sized cubes and toss with olive oil, salt, garlic powder, red pepper flakes and grated Parmesan. Spread bread cubes in a single layer on a baking sheet and bake at 375°F until golden, turning to brown all sides. Remove from oven, and let cool completely.

3. **Arrange salad:** Spoon 4 tablespoons Preserved Lemon Caesar Dressing over warmed brussel sprouts and homemade croutons and toss well. Garnish with shaved parmesan cheese.

# SPICY KALE SALAD
## WITH ROASTED CHICKPEAS & CAULIFLOWER

### INGREDIENTS

1 head cauliflower, separated into florets

15 ounces of chickpeas, drained

olive oil

salt

½ teaspoon cayenne pepper

1 tablespoon cinnamon

1 bunch kale, cut into bite size pieces

1 cup prepared tehina

3 tablespoons lemon juice

1. Place cauliflower and chickpeas on a baking tray and toss with olive oil, salt, cayenne pepper and cinnamon. Bake uncovered at 400°F for 40 minutes.

2. Toss kale with prepared tehina and lemon juice. Mix in roasted cauliflower and chickpeas and let sit for 1 hour before serving.

*My daughter, Allyson, loves to experiment in the kitchen, and these are two of her yummy recipes.*

# ASIAN CHICKEN SALAD

## INGREDIENTS

### Chicken

4-5 dark meat (baby) chicken cutlets marinated in 1 package Good Seasons Italian Seasoning and 2-3 tablespoons sesame oil

### Asian Cole Slaw

1 red onion, chopped
2 tablespoons vegetable oil
4 cloves garlic, crushed
8 ounces shredded red cabbage
8 ounces shredded carrots
¼ pound sugar snap peas
3 tablespoons tamari
3 tablespoons rice vinegar
2 tablespoons sugar
sprinkle of sesame seeds
salt
pepper
pinch of red pepper flakes
2 tablespoons cashews, chopped
1 tablespoon sesame oil

1. Grill seasoned cutlets and cut into thin strips.

2. **Prepare Asian cole slaw:** Over medium heat, sautée red onion in vegetable oil until soft.

   Add garlic then add cabbage, carrots and sugar snap peas and sautée 3-4 minutes until soft. Stir in tamari, rice vinegar, sugar, sesame seeds, salt, pepper and red pepper flakes. Cook 3 minutes.

3. Remove from heat and mix in chicken strips, cashews
   and sesame oil and serve.

# JALAPEÑO CHICKEN SOUP

### INGREDIENTS

1 Vidalia onion, chopped
olive oil
1 jalapeño, seeded and halved
6 cups chicken broth
4 chicken cutlets
salt
pepper
2 tablespoons chopped fresh parsley
Juice of 2 limes
1 avocado, cubed
3 fresh ears of corn, boiled for 8 minutes and remove corn from the cob

1. In a soup pot, sautée onion in olive oil until its edges begin to brown. Add jalapeño and sautée for 2 minutes. Add chicken broth, chicken cutlets, salt and pepper and allow to boil for about 15 minutes or until chicken is cooked through. Discard jalapeños.

2. Remove chicken from pot, cut it into small cubes then return it into the pot. Stir in parsley and lime juice. Return soup to a boil for 1 more minute then remove from heat. Serve topped with cubed avocados and corn.

# MISO SOUP

### INGREDIENTS

24 ounces vegetable broth

6 thin slices of fresh ginger (scrape ginger with a spoon to remove peel then slice off 6 thin slices)

2 tablespoons shiro miso

½ cup sliced mushrooms

¼ teaspoon cayenne pepper

salt

pepper

6-8 Meat Wontons (optional, see recipe page 48)

3 baby bok choy, sliced into bite size pieces

1. Combine vegetable broth, fresh ginger, shiro miso, mushrooms, cayenne pepper, salt and pepper in a large pot over the stove and bring soup to a low boil. Add wontons (if using). Boil soup for 4 minutes.

2. Add bok choy, continue to boil 4-5 minutes and serve.

# SHURBA SOUP

### INGREDIENTS

Hashu Balls (see recipe page 162)

1 Vidalia onion, chopped
Olive oil
2- 15 ounce can tomato sauce
Salt
1 teaspoon cinnamon
½ teaspoon cayenne pepper
water

** This soup should be made in a medium pot to ensure that the hashu balls do not move around too much and fall apart.

In a medium pot, sautée onion in olive oil until its edges begin to golden. Add tomato sauce and one can full of water.

Drop hashu balls into soup then add salt, cinnamon, cayenne pepper and more water to cover hashu balls. Return soup to a low boil for 25 minutes and serve.

# ROASTED ZUCCHINI SOUP

## INGREDIENTS

3 green zucchini, sliced into thin rounds
3 yellow zucchini, sliced into thin rounds
olive oil
salt
pepper
1 Vidalia onion, chopped
½ cup fresh basil, cleaned and dried
½ cup baby spinach
1 jalapeño, seeds removed
32 ounces vegetable broth
1 tablespoon fresh mint

1. Place sliced zucchini on a greased tray and toss with olive oil, salt and pepper. Roast uncovered at 400°F for 20 minutes.

2. In a stock pot, sautée chopped onion in olive oil. Add roasted zucchini (reserving some for garnish), basil, spinach, jalapeño, vegetable broth and mint and boil for 15 minutes. Remove from heat and purée.

May be served chilled or warmed.

** Serve topped with reserved roasted zucchini.

# TOMATO BEAN SOUP

## INGREDIENTS

6 shallots, chopped

olive oil

6 cups water

¾ cup Great Northern Beans, soaked in water for at least 2 hours then drained

16 ounces tomato sauce

1 tablespoon tomato paste

Zest of 1 orange

salt

pepper

½ teaspoon red pepper flakes

2 teaspoons cinnamon

1 head of garlic, cutting off ¼ inch of the top of cloves, exposing the individual cloves of garlic

2 tablespoons chopped fresh mint

1. In a soup pot, sautée shallots in olive oil until their edges begin to golden.

2. **Add to pot:** Water, Great Northern Beans, tomato sauce, tomato paste, orange zest, salt, pepper, red pepper flakes, cinnamon, and garlic head and bring soup to a medium boil.

   Continue to boil soup for 1 ½ hours or until beans are soft yet firm, adding more water if necessary.

3. Squeeze the garlic cloves out of their skins and add them to the soup. Add chopped mint and serve.

# LENTIL SPINACH SOUP

## INGREDIENTS

1 cup butternut squash, chopped into small cubes

1 Vidalia onion, chopped

olive oil

salt

4 cups vegetable broth

4 cups water

½ cup baby lentils, cleaned

pepper

2 cloves garlic, crushed

1 teaspoon cumin

½ teaspoon cayenne pepper

6 ounces baby spinach, chopped

1. **Roast butternut squash:** Arrange butternut squash on a greased baking tray. Season with olive oil and salt and roast in the oven at 400°F for 30 minutes.

2. In a soup pot, sautée onion in olive oil until its edges begin to golden. Add vegetable broth, water and lentils and bring soup to a boil.

   Add salt, pepper, garlic, cumin and cayenne pepper and boil for about 25 minutes until lentils are cooked through yet remain firm.

3. Add roasted butternut squash and spinach to soup and continue to boil 3 minutes more. Adjust seasonings and serve.

# APPETIZERS

Chicken Lettuce Wraps with
Peanut Sauce and Asian Slaw...................................42

Chicken Sliders............................................................45

Lamb Sliders................................................................45

Spinach Ricotta Wontons............................................47

Meat Wontons..............................................................48

Cheese Filled Wontons with Pesto.............................51

Vegetable Wontons.....................................................52

Short Ribs on Sticks...................................................53

Mediterranean Stuffed Tomatoes with Quinoa...........55

Greek Portabella Pizzas..............................................56

Vegetable Portabella Pizzas.......................................57

Crispy Rice with Guacamole and Eggplant Miso....58

Eggplant & Zucchini Chips with Tzatziki.....................60

# CHICKEN LETTUCE WRAPS

## WITH PEANUT SAUCE & ASIAN SLAW

### INGREDIENTS

4 chicken cutlets
3 cups chicken broth

**Asian Slaw**
7 ounces coleslaw
5 ounces shredded red cabbage
slivered almonds (optional)
½ cup craisins

**Dressing**
3 tablespoons soy sauce
3 tablespoons red wine vinegar
¼ cup vegetable oil
1 tablespoon sesame oil
⅓ cup sugar
½ teaspoon red pepper flakes
3 tablespoons peanut butter
4-6 tablespoons water

12-15 Boston lettuce leaves

1. **Prepare chicken cutlets:** On a low fire, boil chicken cutlets in chicken broth for about 15 minutes until cooked through. Remove cutlets and cut into small pieces.

2. **Prepare Asian Slaw:** In a large bowl, combine coleslaw, red cabbage, almonds and craisins. Mix in cut-up chicken pieces.

3. **Prepare dressing:** In a separate bowl whisk together dressing ingredients. (Whisk together until consistency is gravy-like. If too thick, add a few more tablespoons of water).

4. Pour dressing over coleslaw/chicken mixture and toss well. Let marinate at least 30 minutes.

5. Spoon 2 tablespoons of mixture into each piece of Boston lettuce and serve.

### SHAPING AND COOKING SLIDERS:

** Shape sliders according to slider bun. Slider should be slightly bigger than bun. Keep in mind, sliders shrink when cooked.

Form small hamburgers (about 16-20).
** Burgers may be frozen at this point. If not, seal and refrigerate for 2 hours before cooking.

Cooking option #1: Grill burgers on barbeque.
Cooking option #2: Pre-heat oven to 400°F.
In a grill pan over the stove, sear burgers well on both sides then place in oven, uncovered for 10-15 minutes.

# CHICKEN SLIDERS

### INGREDIENTS

1 pound ground dark meat chicken
1 pound ground chicken breast
1 red onion, chopped
1 jalapeño, seeded and chopped
⅓ red chili pepper, seeded and chopped
¼ cup oil
1 tablespoon Sabra S'chug Red mix
3 tablespoons honey
1 teaspoon Montreal Steak Seasoning
2 teaspoons salt

1. Sautée red onion, jalapeño and chili pepper in oil until onion begins to golden.

   Remove from heat and mix in S'chug spice, honey, Montreal steak seasoning and salt. Let cool.

2. Combine onion mixture with ground chicken and mix well with hands to integrate ingredients.

** Serve with Spicy Mayo (see recipe page 175) or Dill Mustard Sauce (see recipe page 183) and Caramelized Onions (see recipe page 179)

# LAMB SLIDERS

### INGREDIENTS

2 pounds extra lean ground lamb
2 shallots, chopped
1 ½ tablespoons oil
2 tablespoon chopped fresh mint
2 tablespoon chopped fresh parsley
zest of 2 lemons
6 tablespoons fresh lemon juice
1 teaspoon red pepper flakes
salt

1. Sautée shallots in oil until its edges begin to golden. Remove from heat and mix in mint, parsley, lemon zest, lemon juice, red pepper flakes and salt.
   Let cool.

2. Combine shallot mixture with ground lamb and mix well with hands to integrate ingredients.

** Lamb Burgers are delicious when served with Caramelized Onions (see recipe page 179)

*I have a new love for these wonton wrappers I discovered. They are very low in calories and are delicious when stuffed with just about anything. Here are a few of my favorites...*

# SPINACH RICOTTA WONTONS

### INGREDIENTS

Square Wonton wrappers, (about 20)

olive oil cooking spray

2 cloves garlic, crushed

olive oil

12 ounces baby spinach

salt

1 cup ricotta cheese

2 tablespoon chopped fresh basil

½ tablespoon chopped fresh mint

10 sundried tomatoes, chopped (may use fresh or jarred in oil)

pepper

1. Sautée garlic in a small amount of olive oil. Add spinach and salt (to taste) and cook until spinach is wilted. Drain well; squeeze out water with a paper towel then let cool.

   Add ricotta, basil, mint, sundried tomatoes, salt and pepper to spinach mixture and mix well.

2. **Assemble:** Lay out one wonton wrapper, keeping the rest covered with a damp cloth so they do not dry out. In the center of the wrapper, place 1 tablespoon of spinach mixture. Spread water over the edges of the wrapper and fold into a triangle. Ensure that edges are tightly sealed by pressing down with a fork.

   ** At this point wontons may be frozen individually for later use.

3. **To bake:** Preheat oven to 400°F. Lay out wontons on a greased baking tray and spray oil cooking spray directly onto wontons. Bake for 15-20 minutes until golden and crisp.

   ** Serve with yogurt topped with fresh mint.

# MEAT WONTONS

### INGREDIENTS

Square Wonton wrappers, (about 30)
olive oil cooking spray
Tadbileh (ground meat filling)
Dipping Sauce

### Tadbileh

1 Vidalia onion, chopped
olive oil
2 jalapeños, seeded and chopped
1 pound chopped meat
salt
2 tablespoons Hot & Spicy ketchup
1 tablespoon Gold's sweet and sour sauce
1 teaspoon Grillmate's Spicy Montreal Steak Seasoning
½ teaspoon cayenne pepper

### Dipping Sauce

¾ cup apricot preserves
⅛ teaspoon cayenne pepper

1. **Prepare Tadbileh:** Sautée onion in olive oil until its edges begin to golden. Add jalapeño and sautée for 2 minutes. Add chopped meat and break up meat with a fork. Add salt. Continue cooking and break up meat until it is browned. Mix in Hot & Spicy ketchup, Gold's sweet and sour sauce, Montreal Steak Seasoning and cayenne pepper and bring to boil 3 minutes until ingredients integrate.

2. **Assemble:** Lay out one wonton wrapper, keeping the rest covered with a damp cloth so they do not dry out. In the center of the wrapper, place 1 tablespoon of Tadbileh. Spread water over the edges of the wrapper and fold into a triangle. Ensure that edges are tightly sealed by pressing down with a fork.

   ** At this point wontons can be frozen individually for later use.

3. **To bake:** Preheat oven to 400°F. Lay out wontons on a greased baking tray and spray oil cooking spray directly onto wontons. Bake for 15-20 minutes until golden and crisp.

4. **Prepare dipping sauce:** In a saucepan, combine apricot preserves and cayenne pepper. Melt down and bring to a boil 2-3 minutes. Remove from heat and serve alongside wontons.

# CHEESE FILLED WONTONS
## WITH PESTO

### INGREDIENTS

Square Wonton wrappers, (about 20-24)
olive oil cooking spray

1 ¾ cup shredded mozzarella cheese
1 egg

Sweet or Lemony Pesto (see recipes page 177)
1 ½ tablespoon chopped fresh oregano
salt
pepper
grated Parmesan cheese
Panko crumbs

1. In a bowl, combine mozzarella and egg and mix well.

2. **Assemble:** Lay out one wonton wrapper, keeping the rest covered with a damp cloth so they do not dry out. In the center of the wrapper, place 1 tablespoon cheese mixture. Spread water over the edges of the wonton and fold them into a triangle. Ensure that edges are tightly sealed by pressing down with a fork.

3. **To bake:** Preheat oven to 400°F. Lay out wontons on a greased baking tray and spray oil cooking spray directly onto wontons.

   Bake for 15-20 minutes until golden and crisp.

   ** Serve drizzled with Sweet or Lemony Pesto (and some extra pesto on the side for dipping).

# VEGETABLE WONTONS

### INGREDIENTS

Square Wonton wrappers, (about 30)
olive oil cooking spray

1 Vidalia onion, chopped
vegetable oil
1 celery stalk, chopped
4 carrots, grated
10-12 white mushrooms, chopped
6 ounces fresh baby spinach, chopped
salt
pepper
1 tablespoon toasted sesame oil
2 tablespoons soy sauce
1 tablespoon agave
½ teaspoon red pepper flakes
vegetable broth

1. In a wide skillet, sautée onion in oil until its edges begin to golden. Add celery, carrots and mushrooms and sautée 5-6 minutes. Add spinach, salt, pepper, sesame oil, soy sauce, agave and red pepper flakes. Stir and continue to sautée until celery is soft yet remains slightly firm.

2. **Assemble:** Lay out one wonton wrapper, keeping the rest covered with a damp cloth so they do not dry out. In the center of the wrapper, place 1 tablespoon vegetable mixture. Spread water over the edges of the wonton and fold them into a triangle.

   Ensure that edges are tightly sealed by pressing down with a fork.

   ** At this point pot stickers may be frozen individually for later use.

3. **To cook:** Coat the bottom of a wide skillet with oil or olive oil cooking spray and heat over the stove. Add pot stickers to skillet (in a single layer) and cook 2-3 minutes until crisp. Flip over pot stickers and add vegetable broth to coat the bottom of the pan (do not allow broth to reach the top, crispy part of the pot sticker). Steam for 2-3 minutes and serve.

   ** **Alternate cooking option:** Pot stickers may be pan fried or sprayed with olive oil cooking spray and baked for 15-20 minutes at 400°F until crisp.

# SHORT RIBS ON STICKS

## INGREDIENTS

20 cubes of flanken (with the bone)

salt

pepper

1 Vidalia onion, chopped

6 cloves garlic, chopped

olive oil

1 cup red wine sweet

½ cup chicken broth

1 tablespoon tomato paste

1 tablespoon Sabra S'chug Hot Red Pepper Mix

8 toothpicks

1. Season flanken with salt and pepper.

2. In a wide skillet, sautée onion in olive oil until its edges begin to golden. Add garlic and sautée for two minutes.

   Remove mixture from pan and add flanken cubes to hot skillet. Sear flanken on both sides until nicely browned. Add to skillet sautéed onion/garlic, red wine, chicken broth, tomato paste and S'chug spice.

3. Cover skillet and transfer to oven, at 350°F for 2 ½ hours or until meat is very tender. Let cool, then skim fat off flanken and discard bones.

   Skewer 3 pieces of meat onto each toothpick, spoon a bit of sauce onto each skewer and serve.

# MEDITERRANEAN STUFFED TOMATOES
## WITH QUINOA

### INGREDIENTS

12-14 ripe plum tomatoes

1 cup quinoa, cooked according to package directions

½ Vidalia onion, chopped

¼ red chili pepper, seeded and chopped

olive oil

8 kalamata olives, chopped

8 sundried tomatoes, chopped

2 tablespoons Sweet or Lemony Pesto, (see recipes page 177)

1 ½ tablespoon chopped fresh oregano

salt

pepper

grated Parmesan cheese

Panko crumbs

1. **Prepare tomatoes:** Core the tomatoes. With a spoon, scoop out tomato seeds and juice and clean the cavities of any clinging seeds. Arrange in a baking dish cut side up.

2. Sautée onion in olive oil until its edges begin to golden. Add chili pepper and sautée for 2 minutes.

3. In a bowl, combine cooked quinoa, sautéed onion/chili pepper, kalamata olives, sundried tomatoes, pesto, oregano, salt and pepper and mix well.

4. Spoon the quinoa into each tomato and sprinkle grated parmesan and panko on top. Arrange stuffed tomatoes in a baking dish, drizzle with olive oil and bake uncovered, at 400°F for 25-30 minutes.

# GREEK PORTABELLA PIZZAS

## INGREDIENTS

4 portabella mushrooms, stems removed and gills scraped

olive oil

Sweet or Lemony Pesto (see recipes page 177)

1 cup baby spinach

feta cheese

6 nicoise olives, chopped

Parmesan cheese, grated

red wine vinegar

dried oregano

1. Brush mushrooms caps with olive oil and arrange, rounded side up, onto an ungreased baking tray. Bake uncovered at 400°F for 20 minutes. Discard any liquids released by the mushrooms.

2. Spread pesto in the cup of the mushrooms cap. Top with spinach, feta, olives and parmesan. Over each pizza, spoon 1 teaspoon vinegar, a sprinkle of dried oregano and a drizzle of olive oil.

3. Bake uncovered at 375°F for 25 minutes.

# VEGETABLE PORTABELLA PIZZAS

## INGREDIENTS

4 portabella mushrooms, stems removed and gills scraped

olive oil

4 round slices of eggplant

4 round slices of vine tomatoes

salt

pepper

sugar

2 cloves garlic, crushed (optional)

4 asparagus spears, cut into ⅓'s (optional)

Your favorite marinara sauce

Mozzarella cheese, grated

1. Brush mushrooms caps with olive oil and arrange, rounded side up, onto an ungreased baking tray. Bake uncovered at 400°F for 20 minutes. Discard any liquids released by the mushrooms.

2. Arrange sliced eggplant and tomatoes on a baking tray and coat with salt, pepper, olive oil and a sprinkle of sugar. Bake uncovered at 400°F for 25 minutes (or until eggplant begins to golden and tomatoes are roasted).

3. **Optional:** In a frying pan, sautée crushed garlic in olive oil for 2 minutes. Add sliced asparagus spears, salt and pepper and sautée 4-5 minutes. Remove from heat.

4. Spread marinara sauce in the cup of the mushrooms cap. Top with a roasted eggplant, followed by a roasted tomato and a sprinkle of mozzarella cheese. If using, arrange chopped asparagus over each pizza, drizzle with olive oil and bake uncovered, at 375°F for 25 minutes.

# CRISPY RICE
## WITH GUACAMOLE AND EGGPLANT MISO

### INGREDIENTS

1 cup sushi rice
1 cup water

**Vinegar water**
⅓ cup rice vinegar
3 tablespoons sugar
1 tablespoon Kosher salt

mini muffin trays
non-stick cooking spray

vegetable oil

1. **Prepare rice:** Combine water and rice in a pot and let sit for 20 minutes. Then, open fire and bring water to a boil. When water evaporates, remove from heat, cover the pot and allow rice to steam for 10 minutes.

2. **Prepare vinegar water:** Combine vinegar water ingredients in a small saucepan and stir over a low fire until sugar dissolves.
Fold mixture gently into cooked rice.

3. **Prepare rice molds:** Pack warm rice into greased muffin trays, pressing down with you fingers to tightly fill the cups.

4. **Crisp the rice:** Invert rice molds to a plate. In a small, deep skillet, heat enough oil to cover the rice mold to an adequate frying temperature (350°F) so that a piece of rice from the mixture actively sizzles when dropped in; alternately, a deep fryer may be used.

Fry the rice 4 to 6 at a time, for about 2-3 minutes, turning as needed to ensure even browning. Drain on paper towels.

**Toppings:**
Spicy Mayo (see recipe page 175)

**Guacamole:**
Combine the following and toss well:
1 avocado, coarsely smashed
½ jalapeño, seeded and chopped
2 tablespoons lemon juice
salt
pepper

**Eggplant Miso:**
½ eggplant, peeled and cubed
olive oil
Combine eggplant and oil and cook together over the stove until eggplant softens; mixing and mashing it as it softens. Add:
2 tablespoons shiro miso
2 tablespoons agave
1 tablespoon mirin
mix and mash together until mixture becomes creamy.

Oven Roasted Tomatoes (see recipe page 181)

5. **To assemble:** Top each piece of crispy rice with a smear of Spicy Mayo. Then, top with either Guacamole or Eggplant Miso with an Oven Roasted Tomato on top.

# EGGPLANT & ZUCCHINI CHIPS
## WITH TZATZIKI

### INGREDIENTS

1 eggplant
1 green zucchini
1 yellow zucchini
salt
pepper
sugar
olive oil cooking spray

**Tzatziki (yogurt dip)**
8 ounces greek yogurt
1 clove garlic, crushed
1 cucumber, diced
salt
pepper
1 teaspoon dried mint leaves

1. Using a mandolin, slice eggplant and zucchini into ¼ inch thick rounds.

2. On a greased baking sheet lay eggplant and zucchini rounds in a single layer. Season with salt, pepper and a sprinkle of sugar.

   Spray cooking spray directly over chips and bake uncovered at 425°F, for 25-30 minutes, watching closely as not to burn chips.

3. **Yogurt dip:** Combine yogurt, garlic, diced cucumber, salt and pepper and mix well.

   Top with dried mint and serve alongside eggplant and zucchini chips.

# SIDES & VEGETABLES

Grilled Corn with Toasted Coconut .............................. 65

Stuffed Artichokes ...................................................... 66

Balsamic Flavored French String Beans ..................... 69

Spaghetti Squash with Vegetables .............................. 70

Crispy Artichokes ....................................................... 73

Shakshuka .................................................................. 74

Potato Galette ............................................................ 76

Eggplant Rollatini with Pesto ...................................... 77

Roasted Butternut Squash with Wasabi Peas ............. 78

Toasted Okra .............................................................. 81

Spinach & White Beans .............................................. 82

String Beans with Flanken .......................................... 84

# GRILLED CORN
## WITH TOASTED COCONUT

### INGREDIENTS

4-6 fresh ears of corn, cut in half

salt

pepper

½ cup shredded sweetened coconut, toasted.
**To toast**
Spread shredded coconut in a thin layer on a baking sheet. Bake at 300°F for about 20 minutes, stirring every 5 minutes to make sure that the coconut browns evenly.

½ cup margarine or Earth Balance™

½ teaspoon cayenne pepper

1 teaspoon salt

½ teaspoon black pepper

2 tablespoons agave

1. **Grilled corn:** Preheat barbeque to high heat. Rub salt and pepper onto corn. Grill corn on the barbeque until they begin to nicely brown on all sides.

2. In a small saucepan melt margarine combined with cayenne pepper, salt, pepper and agave. Roll corn into melted margarine mixture then in toasted coconut and serve.

\*\* The corn can be grilled earlier and just heated for a few minutes right before its rolled in the margarine and toasted coconut.

*Corn may be served whole or cut off the cobs and made into a delicious salad. I like to make this with barbeque and serve corn on sticks.*

# STUFFED ARTICHOKES

## INGREDIENTS

6 artichokes, cleaned and halved

ice water

1 cup lemon juice , divided

### Stuffing

10 shitake mushrooms, stems removed (or any desired mushroom)

1 tablespoon chopped fresh parsley

salt

pepper

1 Vidalia onion, chopped

olive oil

½ cup breadcrumbs

6 Preserved Lemons (see recipe page 171), **cut in fourths**

1. **Clean and prepare artichokes:** Cut off the top third of the artichoke and 1 inch of the stem. Snap off the dark green outer leaves (leaving only the edible yellow leaves). Cut the artichoke in half lengthwise. With a spoon or melon baller, scoop out and discard the hairy choke and thorny inner leaves.

   As you clean artichokes place them in a bowl filled with ice water and ½ cup lemon juice.

   Meanwhile, fill a medium size pot with water and ½ cup lemon juice and bring to a boil. After all artichokes are cleaned, boil them in the water and lemon juice for 4-5 minutes. Remove artichokes from pot, lay them on a paper towel and carefully squeeze to remove excess water.

2. **Prepare stuffing:** In a food processor pulse together shitake mushrooms, parsley, salt and pepper. Set aside.

   Sautée onion in olive oil until its edges begin to golden. Add mushroom/parsley mixture. Add breadcrumbs, salt and pepper and sautée 3 minutes. Remove from heat then mix in preserved lemons.

   Spoon stuffing into artichoke hearts.

   \*\* Stuffed artichokes may be frozen at this point for later use.

3. **To bake:** Lay artichokes in a baking dish (stuffing facing upward), drizzle olive oil over each one and bake uncovered at 350°F for 25 minutes.

# BALSAMIC FLAVORED FRENCH STRING BEANS

### INGREDIENTS

1 ½ pounds French string beans
1 Vidalia onion, chopped
olive oil
3 cloves garlic, crushed
salt
pepper
2 tablespoons sugar
2 tablespoons balsamic vinegar

½ cup panko
zest of 1 lemon
salt
pepper
1 tablespoon chopped fresh parsley

1. In a wide skillet sautée onion in olive oil until its edges begin to golden. Add garlic and sautée for 30 seconds. Add string beans to skillet. Add salt, pepper, sugar and balsamic vinegar. Allow string beans to begin to brown, tossing occasionally.

2. In a dry pan combine panko, lemon zest, salt, pepper and parsley. Mix together and toast until crumbs begin to change color.

3. Transfer string beans to a baking tray and top them with toasted panko mixture. Bake uncovered at 400°F for 10 minutes. Slide string beans onto a platter (trying not to mix in panko) and serve.

*This is a great option for a dietetic, low-calorie dish whose flavor is anything but compromised.*

# SPAGHETTI SQUASH
## WITH VEGETABLES

### INGREDIENTS

1 spaghetti squash, cut in ½ lengthwise
3 cloves garlic, crushed
olive oil
25 cherry tomatoes, halved
salt
pepper
1 cup vegetable broth
6 ounces baby spinach
1 eggplant, cubed
grated mozzarella cheese (optional)

1. **Prepare spaghetti squash:** Place squash face down on a greased baking tray and bake at 350°F for 45 minutes-1 hour. Remove seeds from center of squash and using a fork, scrape out squash strands directly into a bowl.

2. **Prepare vegetables:** In a large skillet, sautée crushed garlic in olive oil. Add cherry tomatoes, salt and pepper and cook 4 minutes. Add vegetable broth and spinach and cook for another 4-6 minutes until spinach is slightly wilted.

   In another skillet, sautée cubed eggplant in olive oil. Add salt and pepper and cook for 10 minutes (until eggplant is soft yet firm – not mushy).

3. Add spaghetti squash to tomato mixture. Add sautéed eggplant, salt and pepper (to taste) and mix well. If not using cheese, warm mixture over the stove and serve.

   When using cheese, arrange mixture into individual dishes or ramekins. Sprinkle grated mozzarella cheese on top and bake at 350°F for 15 minutes.

   Transfer ramekins to the broiler and broil for 5-8 minutes, or until cheese begins to change color.

# CRISPY ARTICHOKES

## INGREDIENTS

4 artichokes, cleaned
ice water
1 cup lemon juice
vegetable oil
3 cloves garlic
3 sprigs fresh thyme
salt
pepper

1. **Prepare artichokes:** Snap off the dark green outer leaves. Cut off the top third of the artichoke and 1 inch of the stem. Using a paring knife peel away the stems tough outer layer and remove the base of the leaves all around (leaving some the yellow, inner, more edible leaves). Cut the artichoke in quarters lengthwise. With a spoon or melon baller, scoop out and discard the hairy choke and thorny inner leaves.

   As you clean artichokes place them in a bowl filled with ice water and lemon juice.

   After all artichokes are cleaned, drain and dry and use them immediately (or freeze them on a tray).

2. Place artichokes face down in a pot. Add oil to top of artichokes. Add garlic, thyme, salt and pepper and fry for 10-15 minutes or until very crispy.

   Remove artichokes from pot, briefly drain on paper towels and serve.

# SHAKSHUKA

### INGREDIENTS

1 Vidalia onion, chopped
olive oil
4 tomatoes, chopped
3 tablespoons tomato sauce
1 teaspoon salt
1 teaspoon allspice
1 teaspoon cinnamon
4 eggs
grated mozzarella cheese, (optional)

1. Sautée onion in olive oil until its edges begin to golden. Add chopped tomatoes, tomato sauce, salt, allspice and cinnamon. Cover and cook on a low flame for 20 minutes.

2. Crack eggs directly on top of tomato mixture, and add a sprinkle of cinnamon and allspice over eggs. If using, add mozzarella cheese over eggs.

   Cover and let cook, about 6 minutes, until egg whites set. (The egg yolk should be still be runny). Serve with toast.

# POTATO GALETTE

### INGREDIENTS

6 white potatoes, peeled and sliced ⅛ inch thin (on a mandolin) and dried well

1 Vidalia onion, cut into thin rounds

1 tablespoon cornstarch

1 tablespoon chopped fresh parsley

1 tablespoon chopped fresh chives

6 tablespoons butter or Earth Balance, melted (divided)

salt

pepper

1. In a mixing bowl, combine potatoes, onions, cornstarch, parsley, chives, 3 tablespoons melted butter, salt and pepper. Mix well.

2. Heat remaining 3 tablespoons butter in a 10 inch non-stick skillet over medium heat.

   Arrange potatoes and onions in an overlapping spiral to fill the pan. Place a medium sauté pan over potatoes to weigh them down and transfer to oven at 450°F for 40 minutes.

   Remove top sauté pan 5-7 minutes before removing skillet from oven.

3. Carefully slide galette onto a platter, cut into wedges and serve.

*As an interesting brunch dish, spread cream cheese over the potato galette and top it with smoked salmon.*

# EGGPLANT ROLLATINI
## WITH PESTO

### INGREDIENTS

#### Eggplant
3 eggplants, cut lengthwise into long thin strips
salt
pepper
sugar
olive oil

#### Cheese mixture
1 cup ricotta cheese
¾ cup shredded mozzarella cheese
1 egg
1 tablespoon chopped fresh parsley
salt
pepper

Pesto (see recipe page 177)
Your favorite marinara sauce

1. **Prepare eggplant:** On a greased baking tray lay eggplant down and sprinkle both sides with salt, pepper, sugar and olive oil. Broil on both sides until golden. (Be careful not to over-broil eggplant, it should be pliable for rolling).

2. **Prepare cheese mixture:** In a bowl combine ricotta cheese, mozzarella, egg, parsley, salt and pepper and mix well.

3. **Assemble rollatini:** Lay eggplant strip on a flat surface and smear 1 heaping teaspoon of pesto on each strip. Place 1 tablespoon cheese mixture on the edge of the eggplant and begin to roll eggplant (roll about 1 ½ times then cut off excess eggplant).

   \*\* Eggplant rollantini may be frozen at this point for later use.

4. Line up rollatini in a greased baking dish and bake uncovered at 400°F for 30 minutes. Carefully arrange rollups onto a platter and serve with a bowl of warmed marinara sauce in the middle.

# ROASTED BUTTERNUT SQUASH
## WITH WASABI PEAS

### INGREDIENTS

1 butternut squash, cubed
vegetable oil
salt
pepper
¼ teaspoon cayenne pepper
1 teaspoon cinnamon
Agave

1 cup wasabi peas, slightly pulsed in a food processor into small pieces
½ cup panko
salt
pepper

1 tablespoon balsamic vinegar
olive oil

1. Arrange cubed butternut squash on a greased baking tray and coat with oil, salt, pepper, cayenne pepper, cinnamon and agave. Bake uncovered at 350°F for 40 minutes, mixing once in between.

2. In a large bowl combine processed wasabi peas, panko, salt and pepper and mix well.

3. Transfer roasted butternut squash to a baking dish or individual ramekins. Coat butternut squash with wasabi/panko topping, drizzle with balsamic vinegar and olive oil and bake uncovered at 400°F for ten minutes. Remove from oven and serve.

# TOASTED OKRA

**INGREDIENTS**

1 pound okra, cut in half legnthwise

olive oil

1 jalapeño, seeded and halved

1 teaspoon salt

¼ cup sesame seeds

¼ Vidalia onion, chopped and sautéed in oil until its edges begin to golden

juice of 1 lemon

1. Coat the bottom of a wide skillet with oil. Heat oil then add okra (in a single layer), jalapeño and salt. Continue cooking about 7 minutes, mixing from time to time while allowing okra to brown in spots.

2. Add sesame seeds and sautéed onion and cook about 8 minutes more, until okra is crispy.

3. Remove from heat and remove jalapeño. Squeeze juice
of 1 fresh lemon over okra and serve.

\*\* If preparing more than the indicated amount, okra should be sautéed in batches.

*Traditionally we are used to cooking a saucy okra, but I experimented and took an instant liking to this variation.*

# SPINACH & WHITE BEANS

## INGREDIENTS

1 Vidalia onion, chopped
3 carrots, cut into thin rounds
olive oil
3 cloves garlic, crushed
15 ounces Cannellini beans
1 teaspoon chopped fresh rosemary
salt
pepper
24 ounces baby spinach, cleaned

1. In a pot, sautée onion and carrots in olive oil on a medium flame until onions edges begin to golden and carrots soften. Add garlic and continue to sautée for 2 minutes.

2. Add Cannellini beans, rosemary, salt and pepper and cook 5-7 minutes. Add spinach and sautée until spinach is just wilted.

*I like to prepare most of this recipe in advance; up to and including sautéing the Cannellini beans. I add the spinach at the last minute so that it does not become too wilted and maintains its bright green color!*

# STRING BEANS
## WITH FLANKEN

### INGREDIENTS

8-10 cubes of flanken
1 Vidalia onion, chopped
olive oil
2 pounds string beans
1 tablespoon cinnamon
salt
2 tablespoons Gold's sweet and sour sauce

1. Sautée chopped onion in oil until its edges begin to golden. Add flanken and brown meat on all sides. Mix in string beans, cinnamon, salt and Gold's sweet and sour sauce.

2. Cover pot and tranfser to oven, at 350°F for 2½ – 3 hours, shaking pot every 45 minutes.

*This is a simple, yet savory recipe which happens to be a perfect Friday night addition.*

# PIZZAS

Grilling a Pizza Dough..............................................88

Arugula Salad Pizza.................................................90

Brussel Sprout Mozzarella Pizza............................93

Grilled Vegetable Pizza...........................................94

# GRILLING A PIZZA DOUGH

## INGREDIENTS

1 frozen ball of dough (may be found in the frozen section of your local supermarket)

flour

cooking spray

Rosemary oil (optional):

olive oil

3 cloves garlic

2 sprigs fresh rosemary

1. **Defrost dough:** Place dough ball in a bowl with flour to coat and allow to thaw out, 4-5 hours.

2. **Hand-stretch pizza dough and grill:** Preheat barbeque and coat with cooking spray. Pick up pizza dough and grab edges between your thumb and index fingers.

   In a circular motion begin stretching the dough. Repeat this circular motion getting the dough as thin as possible without ripping it.

   Place dough directly onto barbeque grates and with your fingers, spread it out into a rectangular shape. Grill for 3-4 minutes (on medium to high heat) or until grill marks appear on the bottom of the dough, then turn over with tongs and repeat process. Remove from barbeque.

3. **Prepare Rosemary Oil (optional):** Coat the bottom of a saucepan with olive oil and add 3 whole garlic cloves and two sprigs of rosemary. Cook on high fire for 3-4 minutes. Remove garlic and rosemary and brush oil over grilled pizza dough for delicious flavor.

   ** At this point pizza can be assembled or bread can be frozen.

These pizza recipes are so easy to make. I love to add these to my weeknight dinners, but mostly when I am entertaining, I love to give my guests a variety of these pizzas.

In these recipes I use store-bought pizza dough. Of course you can make your own pizza dough, but I know when I am preparing a large meal, I always like to cut corners without compromising taste. Here are a few examples of delicious pizzas that present themselves exquisitely.

# ARUGULA SALAD PIZZA

### INGREDIENTS

Grilled pizza dough (see recipe page 88)

Lemony Pesto (see recipe page 177)

Mascarpone cheese

2 cups baby arugula, cleaned

6 fresh figs, halved and drizzled with agave

6 sundried tomatoes, chopped

4 Preserved Lemons, cut into ¼'s (see recipe page 171)

juice of ½ lemon

salt

pepper

1 teaspoon truffle oil or sliced fresh truffles (optional)

1 tablespoon olive oil

Place pizza dough on a baking tray and spread a thin layer of mascarpone cheese over it. Spread a thin layer of lemony pesto over cheese and bake pizza at 350°F for 25 minutes.

Remove from oven and top with baby arugula, followed by figs, sun dried tomatoes, preserved lemons, juice of half of a lemon, salt, pepper and truffle oil or truffles (if using).

Drizzle olive oil over pizza, cut up and serve.

# BRUSSEL SPROUT MOZZARELLA PIZZA

## INGREDIENTS

Grilled pizza dough (see recipe page 88)

### Herbed Ricotta Cheese

1 cup ricotta cheese

½ tablespoon chopped fresh rosemary

1 tablespoon chopped fresh parsley

salt

pepper

¾ cup grated mozzarella cheese

### Brussel Sprouts

1 ½ pounds brussel sprouts, sliced into thin rounds

olive oil

salt

pepper

pinch of red pepper flakes

3 slices Preserved Lemons, cut in ¼'s (see recipe page 171) or 2 lemons, cut in ¼'s

### Caramelized Red Onions

1 red onion, cut into thin rounds

2 tablespoons olive oil

1 tablespoon balsamic vinegar

1. Combine herbed ricotta ingredients and mix well.

2. **Prepare brussel sprouts:** Place brussel sprouts on a greased baking tray and toss with olive oil, salt, pepper and red pepper flakes. Scatter lemons around the tray and bake at 425°F for 20 minutes or until golden.

3. **Caramelize red onions:** In a wide pan, combine olive oil and onions. On a high fire cook onions for 15-20 minutes or until edges begin to brown.

   The last few minutes, add balsamic vinegar and allow it to burn away.

4. **Arrange pizza:** Place grilled pizza dough on a baking tray and spread a layer of herbed ricotta over it. Sprinkle grated mozzarella cheese over ricotta, then add a layer of brussel sprouts (with lemons) and caramelized red onions on top. Sprinkle salt and pepper over pizza.

5. Bake in oven at 350°F for 25 minutes.

# GRILLED VEGETABLE PIZZA

## INGREDIENTS

Grilled pizza dough (see recipe page 88)

Sweet or Lemony Pesto (see recipe page 177)

olive oil

1 Vidalia onion, finely chopped

1 jalapeño, seeded and finely chopped

2 green squash, cubed

2 yellow squash, cubed

salt

pepper

6-8 shiitake mushrooms, cleaned and halved

6-8 dollops of goat cheese

10 sun dried tomatoes, chopped (may use fresh or jarred in oil)

1. In a saucepan, sautée onion in olive oil until its edges begin to golden. Add jalapeño and sautée for 2 minutes. Add cubed squash, salt and pepper and cook until squash is cooked through yet still firm (about 6-8 minutes).

2. **Prepare shiitake mushrooms:** Place halved mushrooms on a greased baking tray. Drizzle with olive oil and bake at 425°F for 25-30 minutes. Remove from oven and add salt.

3. **Arrange pizza:** Place grilled pizza dough on a baking tray and spread a thin layer of pesto over it. Add a layer of sautéed squash and scatter mushrooms on top. Place 6-8 dollops of goat cheese scattered over pizza and sprinkle with chopped sun dried tomatoes.

4. Bake in oven at 350°F for 30 minutes.

# PASTAS & GRAINS

Crispy White Spaghetti..................................................99

Black Rice with Fennel & Pomegranates...................................100

Pasta with Fresh Cherry Tomato Sauce & Melted Mozzarella....102

Quinoa with Roasted Mushrooms & Truffle Oil..........................105

Soba Noodles with a Tehina Sesame Sauce...............................106

Crispy Rice Apricot with Chicken...............................................108

Pasta Bolognese.......................................................................111

# CRISPY WHITE SPAGHETTI

## INGREDIENTS

1 pound pasta (of choice), boiled according to package directions until al dente

½ cup olive oil

3 cloves garlic, crushed

1 teaspoon red pepper flakes

3 tablespoons chopped fresh parsley

2 tablespoons fresh thyme

2 tablespoons chopped fresh chives

¼ cup grated parmesan cheese

1 ½ tablespoons salt

½ cup grated mozzarella cheese

1. In a wide skillet, sautée garlic and red pepper flakes in olive oil. Remove from heat then mix in parsley, thyme, chives, parmesan and salt.

   Add boiled spaghetti to skillet and toss well.

2. Transfer spaghetti mixture to a baking dish and top with grated mozzarella cheese.

3. Broil about 15 minutes until golden, crispy and bubbly.

   ** Be careful not to burn.

# BLACK RICE
## WITH FENNEL & POMEGRANATES

### INGREDIENTS

2 cups blacks rice cooked according to package directions

1 Vidalia onion, chopped

olive oil

1 fennel bulb, cubed

salt

pepper

pinch of red pepper flakes

3 carrots, julienned

¼ cup pomegranate seeds

zest of 1 lemon

juice of 2 lemons

3 tablespoons chopped fresh parsley

1. In a wide skillet, sautée onion in olive oil until its edges begin to golden. Add fennel, salt and pepper and red pepper flakes. Cook for 3-4 minutes.

   Mix in carrots and cook for 2 minutes then remove from heat, leaving vegetables cooked yet still firm and crisp.

2. Combine cooked rice and sautéed vegetables. Mix in pomegranate seeds, lemon zest, lemon juice, chopped parsley and salt and pepper (to taste).

   Serve at room temperature.

*This black rice mixture is also delicious when rolled in grape leaves and baked with a lemon, mint and oil sauce.*

# PASTA WITH FRESH CHERRY TOMATO SAUCE & MELTED MOZZARELLA

### INGREDIENTS

1 box spaghetti, boiled according to package directions until al dente
1 Vidalia onion, chopped
6 cloves garlic, crushed
40 cherry tomatoes, halved
8 ounces tomato sauce
2 tablespoons tomato paste
1 ½ teaspoons dried oregano
1 tablespoon sugar (or 1 Splenda™ packet)
salt
pepper
cubed mozzarella cheese
2-3 tablespoons chopped fresh basil

1. **Prepare tomato sauce:** In a wide saucepan, sautée onion in oil until its edges begin to golden. Add crushed garlic and sautée for 2 minutes.

   Add cherry tomatoes, tomato sauce, tomato paste, oregano, sugar, salt and pepper and cook on a low flame for 15-20 minutes.

2. Add boiled spaghetti to fresh tomato sauce. Add cubed mozzarella and chopped basil and toss together on a low fire for 3 minutes.

*Any variety of mixed mushrooms can be used. My personal favorites are Shiitake, Maitake, and Yellow Oyster mushrooms.*

# QUINOA
## WITH ROASTED MUSHROOMS & TRUFFLE OIL

### INGREDIENTS

1 ½ cups quinoa, cooked according to package directions

2 shallots, chopped

1 Vidalia onion, chopped

olive oil

1 ½ pounds mixed mushrooms, i.e shiitake, maitake and oyster (bigger mushrooms should be cut into large chunks)

Leaves of 1 sprig fresh rosemary, chopped

salt

pepper

6 slices Preserved Lemons (see recipe page 171), cut in ¼'s

Juice of 2 fresh lemons

3 tablespoons chopped fresh parsley

drizzle of truffle oil (or fresh shaved truffles)

3 tablespoons grated parmesan (optional)

1. Sautée shallots and onion together in oil until edges begin to golden.

2. On a greased baking tray, combine mushrooms, sautéed shallots and onions, rosemary, salt and pepper. Liberally oil mushrooms and mix well.

   Scatter preserved lemon quarters around mushrooms. Roast in oven uncovered at 400°F for 40 minutes, tossing twice in between.

3. Mix together cooked quinoa and roasted mushrooms (reserving some mushrooms aside for later use). Mix in lemon juice, parsley, salt and pepper (if needed). Drizzle with truffle oil and add reserved mushrooms on top.

   **Optional:** Sprinkle grated parmesan on top and serve.

# SOBA NOODLES
## WITH TEHINA SESAME SAUCE

### INGREDIENTS

1 pound soba noodles, boiled according to package directions

*Dressing*

5 tablespoons prepared tehina

2 ½ tablespoons soy sauce

2 ½ tablespoons sesame oil

3 tablespoons agave

¼ teaspoon fresh wasabi

½ teaspoon red pepper flakes

3 carrots, grated

1 ear of corn, boiled for 8 minutes then remove corn from the cob

2 tablespoons chopped peanuts

Whisk together dressing ingredients. Pour dressing over boiled soba noodles and toss well. Mix in grated carrots and corn.

Top with chopped peanuts and serve.

*Although there are a lot of steps in this recipe, they are all easy. I do like to make this dish when I have company, and it is always a great complement to a holiday meal!*

# CRISPY RICE
## APRICOT WITH CHICKEN

### INGREDIENTS

**Chicken**

1 whole chicken
¼ cup Gold's sweet and sour sauce
¼ cup orange juice
1 cup water
2 tablespoons oil
paprika
salt

**Brown rice**

4 cups water
1 ½ teaspoons salt
drizzle of oil
2 cups brown rice

**Chopped meat**

1 pound chopped meat
oil
salt
1 tablespoon allspice
1 tablespoon cinnamon
1 Vidalia onion, finely chopped
2 shallots, finely chopped
oil

25 apricots, chopped (divided)
1 bunch fresh parsley, chopped (divided)
salt
pepper
cinnamon

Optional: 3 packages ramen noodles, toasted on a dry pan

1. **Prepare chicken:** Mix together Gold's sweet and sour sauce, orange juice, water and oil and pour over chicken. Season chicken with salt and paprika and massage juice into chicken. Cook covered in oven at 350°F for an hour and 20 minutes. Let cool. Debone chicken then return it into its juices.

2. **Prepare brown rice:** Add water, salt and a drizzle of oil to a small pot over the stove. When water boils add brown rice. Boil for five minutes. Cover and transfer to oven at 350°F for 1 hour.

3. **Prepare chopped meat:** Coat the bottom of wide pan with oil. Add chopped meat and break up meat with a fork. Add salt, allspice and cinnamon. Continue cooking and break up meat until it is browned.

4. **Prepare onions and shallots:** In a small skillet coated with oil, sautée onions and shallots together until lightly browned.

5. **Assemble rice:** In a large pot mix together deboned chicken (and its juice), cooked brown rice, browned chopped meat, sautéed onions and shallots, chopped apricots, chopped parsley (setting aside a handful of both apricots and parsley for later use).

   Add salt, pepper and cinnamon to taste. Bake covered on the bottom rack of the oven at 425°F for 1 hour, or until the bottom of the rice is crisped.

6. Serve topped with toasted ramen noodles (if using) and reserved chopped apricots and parsley.

# PASTA BOLOGNESE

### INGREDIENTS

1 pound white or whole-wheat spaghetti, boiled according to package directions until al dente

#### Bolognese sauce

2 pounds chopped meat, (can be substituted with chopped chicken breast)

1 Vidalia onion, chopped

2 carrots, diced

¼ red pepper, seeded and diced

½ jalapeño, seeded and diced

2 cloves garlic, chopped

olive oil

1 ½ tablespoons cinnamon

salt

pepper

15 ounces tomato sauce

½ cup marinara sauce

½ teaspoon cayenne pepper

2 tablespoons chopped fresh basil

2 tablespoons chopped fresh parsley

¼ cup baby arugula

1. Coat the bottom of a large sautée pan with olive oil. Heat oil then add chopped onion, carrots, red pepper, jalapeño and garlic. Sautée 3-4 minutes. Add chopped meat and break up meat with a fork. Add cinnamon, salt and pepper and continue cooking and break up meat until it is cooked through and browned.

   Mix in tomato sauce, marinara sauce, cayenne pepper, basil and parsley and cook on a low flame for 20-25 minutes. Add arugula and cook 3 minutes more.

2. Arrange cooked spaghetti on a platter and pour bolognese sauce on top.

   ** For a healthier option, this dish can be made with spaghetti squash: 2 spaghetti squash, halved lengthwise and prepared: Place halved squash on a greased baking tray, cut side down.

   Bake at 350°F for 40 minutes.

   With a spoon, scoop out squash seeds. Then with a fork, scrape out spaghetti squash into a platter. Pour Bolognese sauce on top and serve.

# FISH

Blackened Grouper with Mango Corn Salsa........................114

Panko Crusted Tuna with Spicy Mayo.................................116

Grilled Salmon with Dill Sauce............................................119

Sea Bass Lettuce Cups with Shredded Fillo........................121

Slow Roasted Halibut........................................................122

# BLACKENED GROUPER
## WITH MANGO CORN SALSA

### INGREDIENTS

3-6 ounce pieces of grouper, butterflied
Spicy Mayo (see recipe page 175)

salt

pepper

2 tablespoons chopped fresh oregano

½ packet Good Seasons Italian Seasoning

¼ teaspoon cayenne pepper

½ teaspoon cumin

cooking spray

#### Mango Corn Salsa

4 ears of corn, boiled for 8 minutes and remove corn off the cob

2 mangos, cubed

2 avocadoes, cubed

20 cherry tomatoes, halved

½ jalapeño, seeded and chopped

olive oil

3 tablespoons lime juice

salt

pepper

1. **Preparing and grilling the grouper:** Coat barbeque with cooking spray and preheat barbeque. In a small bowl combine salt, pepper, oregano, ½ packet Italian seasoning, cayenne pepper and cumin and mix well.

   Brush each piece of grouper with spicy mayo then dip fish into seasonings mixture. Barbeque fish on a high flame for 5-7 minutes on each side.

2. **Mango corn salsa:** In a bowl, combine corn, mango, avocado and cherry tomatoes. Add jalapeño, olive oil, lime juice salt and pepper and toss.

3. Serve grouper topped with Mango Corn Salsa.

# PANKO CRUSTED TUNA
## WITH SPICY MAYO

### INGREDIENTS

2- 6 ounce tuna steaks, cut in 3 long pieces against the grain

sesame teriyaki

1 cup panko

Olive oil

**Spicy Mayo** (see recipe page 175)

1. Roll tuna in sesame teriyaki, then bread it in panko.

2. Heat a thin layer of olive oil in a wide skillet over medium heat until very hot. Add tuna and cook for 30 seconds on each of its 4 sides.

   ** For well done fish, cook for 1 minute on each side.

3. Remove fish from skillet and with a sharp knife, cut into 1 inch pieces, resembling sushi bites.

   Dip in spicy mayo and enjoy!

*This dish resembles sushi bites and brings sushi to your own kitchen!*

# GRILLED SALMON
## WITH DILL SAUCE

### INGREDIENTS

1 side of salmon, skin removed
2 tablespoons chopped fresh parsley
2 tablespoons chopped fresh chives
1 tablespoon chopped fresh rosemary
¼ cup honey
¼ cup soy sauce
1 tablespoon Dijon mustard
3 cloves garlic, crushed
cooking spray

#### Topping
1 cup cornflake crumbs
⅓ cup sesame seeds
2 tablespoons slivered almonds
½ cup brown sugar
2 tablespoons vegetable oil

1. In a resealable sandwich bag, combine salmon with parsley, chives, rosemary, honey, soy sauce, mustard and garlic. Marinate in refrigerator from as little as 3 hours to overnight.

2. Preheat barbeque grill to high and coat with cooking spray. Place salmon onto barbeque and grill 3-4 minutes. Using 2 spatulas, carefully flip salmon and grill for another 3-4 minutes. Remove from barbeque and transfer to a baking tray. (Salmon should still be rare at this point).

3. Rub directly onto top of salmon: Cornflake crumbs, sesame seeds, slivered almonds, brown sugar and vegetable oil and bake in oven at 425°F for 10 minutes.

\*\* Serve with Dill Mustard Sauce on the side (See recipe page 183).

# SEA BASS LETTUCE WRAPS
## WITH SHREDDED FILLO

### INGREDIENTS

1 pound sea bass, butterflied and cut into 2 inch cubes

¼ cup soy sauce

2 tablespoons honey

1 tablespoon brown sugar

1 teaspoon sesame oil

½ teaspoon cayenne pepper

1 tablespoon prepared tehina

8 ounces shredded fillo dough

Boston lettuce

1. Marinate sea bass in soy sauce, honey, brown sugar, sesame oil, cayenne pepper and prepared tehina. Marinate for as little as 6 hours or up to overnight.

2. **Prepare and toast shredded fillo:** Gently shake fillo dough to loosen ¼ of the dough. Toast dough in a greased pan over the stove (moving it around frequently to ensure that all parts of the dough are toasted).

3. Preheat oven to broil. Lay marinated sea bass cubes (eliminating excess marinade) on a greased tray and broil in oven 10-15 minutes or until fish begin to brown in spots.

4. Arrange a sea bass cube in each Boston lettuce cup, top with toasted shredded fillo and serve.

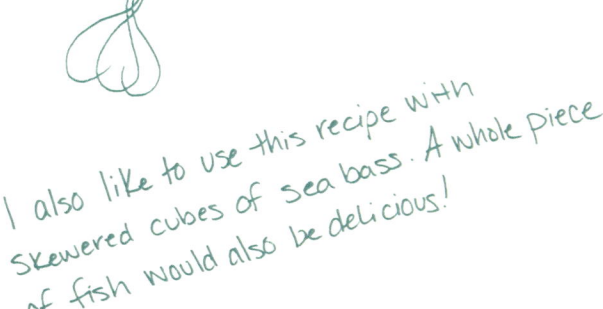

I also like to use this recipe with skewered cubes of sea bass. A whole piece of fish would also be delicious!

# SLOW ROASTED HALIBUT

### INGREDIENTS

4 pieces of Halibut (with the bone)

4 tablespoons slivered almonds

4 slices Preserved Lemons (see recipe page 171)

3 teaspoons capers

4 tablespoons extra virgin olive oil

½ cup lemon juice (preferably taken from the preserved lemon jar)

1. Preheat oven to 300°F.

2. Heat a dry skillet over the stove. Spread almonds across the pan in a thin even layer. Stir or shake the pan frequently to prevent the almonds from burning.

   Just before the almonds begin to develop browned edges, add lemons to the pan and cook for 2 minutes. Remove from heat and add capers, olive oil and lemon juice. Allow mixture to cool.

3. Arrange fish on a greased baking dish. Pour almond and lemon juice mixture over fish and bake fish uncovered, for 20-25 minutes. Then place under broiler for 2 minutes. Transfer cooked fish onto a platter, spoon 1 tablespoon of its juice over each piece, and serve with remaining juice alongside the fish.

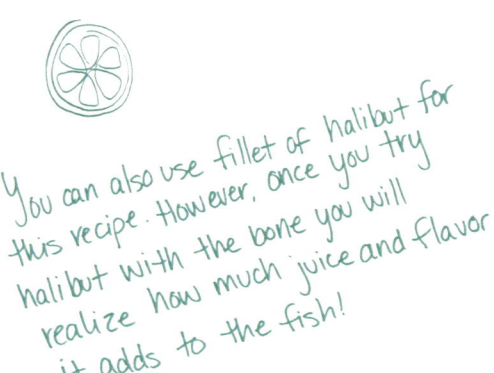

*You can also use fillet of halibut for this recipe. However, once you try halibut with the bone you will realize how much juice and flavor it adds to the fish!*

# CHICKEN

Baby Chicken Over French String Beans..................................126

Tamarind Chicken with Roasted Fingerling Potatoes.............129

Eggplant Chicken Pie............................................................130

Spinach Chicken Burgers......................................................133

Roasted Herb-Spiced Cornish Hens.......................................134

Broiled Eggplant Chicken Wrap..............................................137

# BABY CHICKEN
## OVER FRENCH STRING BEANS

### INGREDIENTS

8 skinless boneless baby chicken thighs
2 tablespoons chopped fresh basil
2 tablespoons chopped fresh parsley
2 tablespoons chopped fresh rosemary
¼ cup soy sauce
1 ½ tablespoons sesame oil
3 cloves garlic, crushed
½ teaspoon red pepper flakes
2 tablespoons agave
3 tablespoons olive oil

2 pounds French string beans
olive oil
2 cloves garlic, crushed
⅓ cup soy sauce
1 teaspoon sesame oil
2 tablespoons agave

1. **Marinate chicken:** Combine basil, parsley, rosemary, soy sauce, sesame oil, crushed garlic, red pepper flakes, agave and olive oil and mix well.

   Pour over chicken and marinate overnight in a resealable sandwich bag.

2. **Prepare string beans:** Coat the bottom of a wide skillet with olive oil. Add French string beans and sautée for 4 minutes. Mix in garlic and cook for 2 minutes. Add soy sauce, sesame oil and agave and cook for another 3-4 minutes.

   Do not overcook; string beans should be crispy.

3. **Grill chicken:** In a greased grill pan, grill chicken on both sides (6-7 minutes on each side, lowering the flame if the outside of the chicken begins to burn) until chicken is cooked through.

4. Assemble string beans on a platter with grilled chicken on top and serve.

# TAMARIND CHICKEN
## WITH ROASTED FINGERLING POTATOES

### INGREDIENTS

2 pounds fingerling potatoes, cut in half lengthwise

olive oil

salt

pepper

6 pieces chicken leg and thigh (or 1 whole chicken)

salt

pepper

paprika

3 cloves garlic, crushed

9 tablespoons tamarind, divided

½ cup cranberry juice

½ cup orange juice

3 tablespoons agave

3 tablespoons vegetable oil

6 Preserved Lemons (see recipe page 171)

1. On a greased baking tray, place fingerling potatoes and toss with olive oil, salt and pepper. Roast uncovered at 400°F for 45 minutes – 1 hour, tossing twice in between.

2. Place cleaned chicken in a large roaster. Massage salt, pepper, paprika and crushed garlic into chicken.

3. In a separate bowl mix together 6 tablespoons tamarind, cranberry juice, orange juice, agave and oil. Pour juice over chicken.

   Scatter Preserved Lemons over chicken pieces.

4. Spoon the remaining 3 tablespoons tamarind over chicken and bake covered, at 425°F for 30 minutes.

   Uncover and bake for 20 minutes. Add roasted potatoes around chicken and bake for another 30 minutes, (watching chicken closely so as not to overcook it).

# EGGPLANT CHICKEN PIE

## INGREDIENTS

### Eggplant
2 eggplant, sliced into thin rounds
salt
pepper
sugar
olive oil

### Brown rice
4 cups water
1 ½ teaspoons salt
drizzle of oil
2 cups brown rice

### Chicken
1 whole chicken
¼ cup Gold's sweet and sour sauce
¼ cup orange juice
2 tablespoons oil
paprika
salt
pepper

1 tablespoon salt
1 teaspoon allspice
1 tablespoon cinnamon
cooking spray

1. **Prepare eggplant:** On a greased baking tray lay eggplant and sprinkle both sides with salt, pepper, sugar and olive oil. Broil slightly on both sides until eggplant begins to golden, being careful to not overcook eggplant.

    ** Eggplant may be prepared in advance and frozen for later use.

2. **Prepare brown rice:** Add water, salt and a drizzle of oil to a small pot over the stove. When water boils, add brown rice. Boil for five minutes on the clock. Cover and transfer to oven at 350°F for 1 hour.

3. **Prepare chicken:** Mix together Gold's sweet and sour sauce, orange juice and oil and pour over chicken. Season chicken with paprika, salt and pepper and massage juice into chicken. Cook covered in oven at 350°F for 1 ½ hours.

    Let cool. Debone chicken then return it to its juices.

4. Add cooked rice to deboned chicken and its juice Add salt, allspice and cinnamon and mix together.

5. Line the bottom of wide non-stick skillet (coated with cooking spray) with half of the broiled eggplant. Add rice/chicken mixture and lay the other half of the eggplant on top of the rice.

6. Bake covered at 425°F for 1 hour and 45 minutes. Turn pie over into a platter and serve.

# SPINACH CHICKEN BURGERS

## INGREDIENTS

1 ½ pounds ground chicken breast
1 ½ pounds ground dark meat chicken
1 Vidalia onion, chopped
vegetable oil
1 jalapeño, seeded and diced
18 ounces fresh baby spinach
salt
1 teaspoon Sabra S'chug Red Pepper Mix

1. Sautée onion in oil until its edges begin to golden. Add jalapeño and sautée for two minutes. Add spinach, salt and Sabra S'chug mix and continue to cook until spinach begins to wilt. Drain spinach. Let cool, then with a knife, slightly chop up spinach mixture.

2. Combine spinach mixture with chopped chicken, add salt to mixture and mix well with hands to integrate ingredients. Form burgers, 3 inches in diameter (about 18 burgers).

   ** Burgers may be frozen at this point. If not, seal and refrigerate for 2 hours before cooking.

3. **Cooking option #1:** Grill burgers on barbeque.
   **Cooking option #2:** Pre-heat oven to 400°F.

   In a grill pan over the stove, sear burgers well on both sides then place in oven, uncovered for 10-15 minutes.

# ROASTED HERB-SPICED CORNISH HENS

## INGREDIENTS

3 cornish hens, cut in half
5 cloves garlic, crushed
1 tablespoon chopped fresh basil
1 tablespoon chopped fresh oregano
2 tablespoons chopped fresh parsley
(or any mix of chopped fresh herbs i.e thyme, chives, mint etc.)
zest of 3 lemons
salt
pepper
paprika
olive oil
6 tablespoons Gold's sweet & sour sauce

1. Massage garlic, basil, oregano, parsley, lemon zest, salt, pepper, paprika and olive oil into chicken.

2. Place herbed chicken in a roaster and spoon 1 tablespoon Gold's sweet & sour sauce over each piece of chicken.

   Bake chicken covered, on the second shelf from the top of the oven, for 50 minutes at 425°F.

   Uncover and bake for 25 minutes.

# BROILED EGGPLANT CHICKEN WRAP

### INGREDIENTS

16 chicken cutlets flat or baby chicken cutlets (wider chicken cutlets should be cut in half lengthwise)

#### Eggplant

3 eggplant, cut lengthwise into long thin strips

salt

pepper

sugar

otlive oil

Hashu (see recipe page 162)

#### Sauce

3 tablespoons duck sauce

¼ cup orange juice

2 tablespoons vegetable oil

¼ cup water

1. **Prepare eggplant:** On a greased baking tray, lay eggplant down and sprinkle both sides with salt, pepper, sugar and olive oil. Broil on both sides until golden. (Be careful not to over-broil eggplant, it should be pliable for rolling).

2. **Assemble rollups:** Lay chicken cutlet on a flat surface. Spoon 1 tablespoon Hashu onto the edge of each cutlet and roll up. Wrap each piece of rolled chicken in a slice of broiled eggplant.

3. **Prepare sauce:** In a small bowl, combine duck sauce, orange juice, oil and water. Mix well.

4. Lay roll-ups in a wide skillet, in a single layer. Pour sauce over roll-ups and bake covered at 350°F for 40 minutes. Remove cover and bake another 20 minutes. Carefully arrange rollups onto a platter and serve.

# MEAT

Tangy Meat Tacos..................................................................................141

Balsamic Glazed Rack of Lamb with Espresso Rub..................142

Breaded Rack of Lamb with Dijon & Rosemary.........................144

Minute Steak Split...................................................................145

Eggplant & Meatballs..............................................................147

Lamb Riblets...........................................................................148

Lorraine Gindi's Rack of Veal with a Lemon Wine Sauce...........151

Meat Stuffed Artichokes..........................................................152

Pepper Crusted Fillet Mignon..................................................154

Veal Scallopini with a Tomato Mushroom Sauce......................156

Korean Short Ribs...................................................................159

French Cut Roast....................................................................160

Hashu (Meat & Rice Stuffing)..................................................162

Veal Pocket Neck with Peas and Hashu...................................163

Japanese Vegetable Bowl.......................................................165

*Sometimes I like to serve this dish as an appetizer. I simply place taco meat on toasted, low-calorie wontons, top them with avocado and preserved lemons, and serve!*

# TANGY MEAT TACOS

### INGREDIENTS

12 small flour tortillas

Preserved lemons (see recipe page 171), cut in ¼'s

##### Meat

2 pounds chopped meat

1 Vidalia onion, chopped

olive oil

1 ½ jalapeños, seeded and chopped

1 tablespoon salt

1 teaspoon allspice

1 teaspoon cinnamon

##### Sauce

½ cup yellow mustard

¼ cup sugar

¼ cup brown sugar

⅛ teaspoon cayenne pepper

⅓ cup rice vinegar

2 tablespoons A1™ Bold and Spicy steak sauce

2 tablespoons whiskey

##### Avocado topping

1 avocado, cut into small cubes

2 tablespoons olive oil

salt

red pepper flakes

juice of 1 fresh lemon

1. **Bake tortillas:** Drape each tortilla directly over two bars of your oven rack. Bake at 400°F, for about 4-5 minutes, until tortillas begin to hold shape.

   \*\* Tortillas can be prepared in advance and heated up prior to stuffing and serving them.

2. **Prepare meat:** Sautée onion in olive oil until its edges begin to golden. Add jalapeño and sautée for 2 minutes. Add chopped meat and break up meat with a fork.

   Add salt, allspice and cinnamon and continue cooking and finely break up meat until meat is browned.

   Add sauce ingredients directly onto browned meat and mix well. Allow ingredients to integrate and bring to a low boil for 10 minutes. Remove from heat.

3. **Prepare Avocado topping:** Combine avocado topping ingredients and toss.

4. **Arrange tacos:** Stuff tacos with 3 tablespoons of meat topped with avocado and preserved lemons. Eat and enjoy!

# BALSAMIC GLAZED RACK OF LAMB
## WITH ESPRESSO RUB

### INGREDIENTS

1 rack of lamb

*Rub*

3 tablespoons brown sugar
2 tablespoons espresso instant coffee
salt
pepper

*Glaze*

½ cup balsamic vinegar
¼ cup sweet red wine
3 tablespoons agave
1 teaspoon Dijon mustard
2 sprigs fresh rosemary

1. Mix together rub ingredients and massage onto rack of lamb. Wrap rack of lamb tightly in a plastic wrap and marinate in refrigerator for at least 4 hours and up to 2 days.

2. In a small pot over the stove, combine glaze ingredients. Bring to a boil and reduce to half until syrupy, 5-8 minutes.

3. Transfer lamb to a baking tray lined with parchment paper, pour glaze over it and cook in oven uncovered, at 350°F for 40-45 minutes.

Slice and serve.

# BREADED RACK OF LAMB
## WITH DIJON & ROSEMARY

### INGREDIENTS

1 rack of lamb
2 tablespoons Dijon mustard
pepper
chopped fresh rosemary

½ cup bread-crumbs
zest of ½ lemon

1. Smear a thin layer of Dijon mustard over rack of lamb. Sprinkle pepper over Dijon and top with chopped rosemary.

2. In a separate bowl, combine bread-crumbs and lemon zest and mix well. Sprinkle mixture over rack of lamb.

3. Transfer lamb to a baking tray lined with parchment paper and cook uncovered in the oven, at 350°F for 40-45 minutes.

    Slice and serve.

# MINUTE STEAK SPLIT

### INGREDIENTS

1 minute steak split
salt
Grill Mates Montreal Steak Seasoning
brown sugar
olive oil

3 cups orange juice
4 tablespoons A1 steak sauce
5 tablespoons Worcestershire sauce
5 tablespoons honey

2-3 white sweet potatoes, cut into thin rounds (leaving peel on)
olive oil
salt

1. **Sear minute steak:** Rub salt, Montreal Steak Seasoning and brown sugar onto both sides of minute steak.

   Heat oil in a large grill pan over the stove. When oil is hot, add minute steak to the pan and sear nicely on both sides (4-5 minutes on each side) until grill marks appear.

2. **Prepare sauce:** In a small pot over the stove, combine orange juice, A1™ steak sauce, worchestire sauce and honey. Boil to simmer, stirring frequently for about 30 minutes, until sauce thickens and is able to coat the back of a spoon.

3. **Prepare potato chips:** On a greased baking tray, lay potatoes coated with oil and salt. Bake uncovered at 425°F for 45 minutes.

4. **Assemble:** (Reserving ½ cup of the prepared sauce) Place potatoes and remaining sauce into a wide skillet. Transfer skillet to oven and bake covered, at 350°F for 25 minutes. Remove from oven, add seared meat over the potatoes and transfer skillet to the broiler for 15 minutes. Steak should be pink inside and read 140°F on a meat thermometer.

\*\* Serve potatoes with sliced meat on top.

Heat extra juice and pour over meat.

# EGGPLANT & MEATBALLS

## INGREDIENTS

### Eggplant
1 eggplant, sliced into thin rounds
salt
pepper
sugar
olive oil

### Meatballs
1 pound chopped meat

3 potatoes, cubed and processed in food processor until they become fluffy and airy. (In this recipe, we only use half the amount of our processed potatoes. However, if we process less than 3 potatoes, they do not become airy)

⅓ cup matzo meal

1 teaspoon salt

### Barbeque Sauce
1 Vidalia onion, chopped
½ cup chili sauce
1 jalapeño, seeded and chopped
½ teaspoon red pepper flakes
⅓ cup ketchup
1 tablespoon Worcestershire sauce
1 teaspoon Dijon mustard
1 teaspoon red wine vinegar
2 tablespoons water

Oven Roasted Tomatoes
(optional, see recipe page 181)

1. **Prepare eggplant:** On a greased tray, lay eggplant and sprinkle both sides with salt, pepper, sugar and olive oil. Broil on both sides until golden, being careful to not overcook eggplant.

    ** Eggplant may be prepared in advance and frozen for later use.

2. **Prepare meatballs:** Combine chopped meat, ½ of the processed potatoes, matzo meal and salt and mix well with hands. Form balls, around 2 inches in diameter.

    ** Meatballs may be prepared in advance and frozen for later use.

3. **Prepare barbeque sauce:** In a small pot, combine barbeque sauce ingredients and bring to a boil for 1 minute.

4. **Arrange:** Line broiled eggplant on the bottom of a greased baking dish. Lay a meatball over each piece of eggplant and top with 1 ½ tablespoons of barbeque sauce.

    Cover and bake at 350°F for 45 minutes.

5. Uncover and bake for another 20-25 minutes. (If adding Oven Roasted Tomatoes, place 1 tomato over each meatball for the last 10 minutes of baking).

# LAMB RIBLETS

## INGREDIENTS

4 strips lamb rib ends (this is the strip that comes on the bottom of a rack of lamb)

### Dry rub

salt
pepper
2 tablespoons brown sugar
1 teaspoon red pepper flakes

4 tablespoons hoisin sauce
2 cloves garlic, crushed
2 tablespoons honey

1. Combine rub ingredients in a bowl and mix well. Smear dry rub over lamb riblets, place riblets in a roaster, cover tightly with plastic wrap and marinate overnight in refrigerator.

2. Transfer lamb to wide skillet, cover and bake at 250°F for 3 hours or until very tender.

3. In a small bowl combine hoisin sauce, garlic and honey and mix well.

   Brush lamb with mixture and return to oven at 425°F until glaze begins to caramelize (about 5 minutes).

# LORRAINE GINDI'S
# RACK OF VEAL
## WITH A LEMON WINE SAUCE

### INGREDIENTS

1 rack of veal

2 tablespoons spicy mustard

2 tablespoons McCormick Grill Mates Onion and Garlic Medley

2 tablespoons vegetable oil

1 tablespoon Kosher salt

#### Lemon Wine Sauce

3 cups chicken broth (or Imagine No Chicken Broth)

½ cup white wine (Chablis or any dry white wine)

¾ cup fresh lemon juice

1 tablespoon Osem Chicken Consomme

2 tablespoons chopped fresh parsley

1 teaspoon corn starch mixed with ¼ cup cold water

1. In a small bowl, mix together mustard, McCormicks Onion and Garlic Medley, vegetable oil and Kosher salt.

2. Rub mixture over rack of veal and bake uncovered (in a tray with a 3 inch lip), for 1 ½ hours or until desired temperature is reached. Slice and serve with lemon wine sauce.

    ** It is always beneficial to measure the temperature of the meat to ensure it is cooked to your desire.

    For medium rare thermometer should read 135°F, medium 140°F, and well done 165°F.

    I personally love my meat at about 137°F where it is pink inside, yet cooked and very tender.

3. **Lemon Wine Sauce:** In a small saucepan, combine chicken broth, white wine, lemon juice, chicken consommé and parsley.

    Cook on a low fire, stirring frequently, for about 45 minutes. Stir in cornstarch and cook for another 5 minutes.

    ** Serve alongside sliced rack of veal.

# MEAT STUFFED ARTICHOKES

### INGREDIENTS

2 pounds ground chopped meat
1 Vidalia onion, chopped
olive oil
½ jalapeño, seeded and chopped
1 teaspoon salt
1 teaspoon cinnamon
2 tablespoons chili sauce
½ teaspoon cayenne pepper

28- 30 artichoke bottoms or fresh artichokes cleaned (as in recipe for Stuffed Artichokes. See recipe page 66)
1 cup cornflake crumbs

### Sauce

6 tablespoons tamarind
¼ cup tomato sauce
1 teaspoon salt
4 tablespoons sugar
4 tablespoons vegetable oil
½ cup water

1. Sautée onion and jalapeño in oil until edges it edges begin to golden. Let cool.

2. Combine raw chopped meat, sautéed onion/jalapeño, salt, cinnamon, chili sauce and cayenne pepper and mix well with hands to integrate ingredients.

3. Stuff artichoke bottoms with meat mixture and dip meat into corn-flake crumbs.

   ** Stuffed artichokes may be frozen at this point.

4. Combine artichoke sauce ingredients and mix well.

5. In a large skillet arrange artichokes in a single layer, corn-flake crumbs face up. Pour sauce over each artichoke individually, pouring remaining sauce to cover the bottom of the skillet.

   Bake covered at 350 °F for 1 hour. Uncover and bake for 20 minutes.

# PEPPER CRUSTED FILLET MIGNON

## INGREDIENTS

4 fillet mignon
Peppercorns, crushed

2 shallots, diced
olive oil
½ cup sweet red wine
4 tablespoons balsamic vinegar
½ cup chicken broth
1 teaspoon cornstarch

meat thermometer

1. Roll fillet mignon in crushed black peppercorns. Over the stove, heat a dry cast iron skillet. Add steaks to hot skillet and sear on both sides (about 4-5 minutes on each side).

2. In a separate pot sautée shallots in olive oil. Add wine, balsamic vinegar and chicken broth and boil until reduced to half (7-8 minutes).

   Sprinkle in cornstarch and whisk together for 1 minute, until mixture slightly thickens. (Mixture should not be as thick as gravy. If so, add water for thinner consistency).

3. Add sauce mixture to seared steaks in the grill pan. Place uncovered pan in oven, at 400°F, for 10-15 minutes, or until internal temperature reaches 130°F for medium-rare steak and 137°F for medium steak.

4. Remove steaks from oven, cover loosely and let sit for 10 minutes before serving.

# VEAL SCALLOPINI
## WITH A TOMATO MUSHROOM SAUCE

### INGREDIENTS

8 veal scallopini
2 eggs
3 cloves garlic, crushed
salt
pepper
Panko
zest of 3 lemons
2 tablespoons chopped fresh parsley
vegetable oil

#### Tomato Mushroom Sauce
1 shallot, chopped
olive oil
1 box sliced white mushrooms
salt
pepper
red pepper flakes
⅓ cup sweet red wine
2 cups of your favorite marinara sauce
2 tablespoons chopped fresh parsley

1. In a large bowl whisk together eggs, garlic, salt and pepper. Add veal to mixture, cover with plastic wrap and marinate in refrigerator for as little as 1 hour up to overnight.

2. In a separate bowl, mix together panko, lemon zest, chopped fresh parsley, salt and pepper. Bread each piece of veal in panko mixture.

3. **Cooking option #1:** Heat oil in a wide pan over the stove. Add breaded veal and fry until nicely golden on each side.

   **Cooking option #2:** Arrange veal on a greased baking tray, drizzle with vegetable oil and bake uncovered, at 400°F for 20-25 minutes.

4. **Prepare tomato mushroom sauce:** Sautée chopped shallots in olive oil until nicely browned. Over high heat, add sliced white mushrooms, salt, pepper and red pepper flakes and continue to sautée 3 minutes. Mix in sweet red wine and bring mixture to a boil.

   Deglaze pan and continue to cook until mixture is reducedto half. Add your favorite marinara sauce, chopped parsley, salt, pepper and simmer for 7-10 minutes.

** Serve warmed sauce over or alongside veal scallopini.

# KOREAN SHORT RIBS

### INGREDIENTS

10- 3 bone short ribs
½ cup soy sauce
4 tablespoons sesame oil
3 tablespoons rice vinegar
¼ cup brown sugar or agave
3 tablespoons sesame seeds
½ teaspoon red pepper flakes
4 scallions, chopped
5 cloves garlic, crushed

cooking spray

1. Place short ribs in a double bagged 2 gallon resealable sandwich bag. In a bowl combine soy sauce, sesame oil, rice vinegar, sugar, sesame seeds, red pepper flakes, scallions and crushed garlic. Mix well then pour over short ribs. Marinate from as little as overnight to up to two days.

2. Coat barbeque with cooking spray and preheat barbeque. Reserving the sauce for later use, grill short ribs on one side until grill marks appear (4-5 minutes). Turn over and repeat process

   Transfer short ribs to a baking dish or roaster in a single layer. Spoon 1 tablespoon of sauce over each rib, cover and cook at 325°F for 1 ½- 2 hours.

# FRENCH CUT ROAST

### INGREDIENTS

1.5 pound french cut roast
salt
pepper
2 cloves garlic, crushed
1 cup mustard (of choice)
3 tablespoons brown sugar
1 tablespoon oil

### Caramelized Peppers

1 red pepper, cut into strips
1 yellow pepper, cut into strips
3 tablespoons olive oil

**Caramelized Onions** (see recipe page 179)

meat thermometer
1 loaf French bread, sliced open and warmed

1. **Marinate roast:** Mix together salt, pepper, garlic, mustard, brown sugar and oil and rub onto roast. Wrap tightly in plastic wrap and marinate overnight in refrigerator.

2. **Prepare caramelized peppers:** In a wide pan combine peppers and olive oil. Cook over the stove on a high fire for 15-20 minutes or until peppers turn a golden brown color.

3. **Prepare barbeque:** Remove roast from refrigerator 2 hours before barbequing. Heat both sides of the barbeque grill to high heat. When they have reached high heat, completely close one side of the grill.

4. **Barbeque roast:** Lay roast directly onto the heated side of the grill, searing for 4-5 minutes. Flip roast over and sear for another 4-5 minutes. Transfer and loosely wrap roast in a single layer of aluminum foil. Place wrapped meat back on the barbeque but on the closed side of the grill.

   Close top of barbeque and cook for 25-35 minutes, checking with a meat thermometer until meat reaches 140°F.

5. Remove from barbeque and let meat rest for 10 minutes. Slice into thin pieces with an electric knife, reserving all juices that are let out from the meat.

6. Arrange meat over warmed French bread. Top with caramelized peppers and onions, pour juices over meat and serve.

# HASHU
## (MEAT & RICE STUFFING)

### INGREDIENTS

½ cup short grain Goya™ rice
½ cup water
1 teaspoon salt
1 teaspoon oil

1 pound chopped meat
1 teaspoon salt
1 tablespoon allspice
½ tablespoon cinnamon
¼ cup cold water

1. **Parboil water and rice:** In a pot on a high flame, add equal amounts of water and rice. Add salt and oil. When water boils, lower the flame and let rice cook until all water evaporates. Remove from heat and let cool.

2. Combine parboiled rice with chopped meat then add salt, allspice, cinnamon and cold water. Mix well.

3. When making Hashu balls, this filling should be formed into balls and frozen on a tray.

   ** (Hashu balls should be prepared in advance and frozen).

   ** Hashu should be used with Shurba Soup (see recipe page 35), Veal Neck Pocket with Peas (see recipe page 163) and Broiled Eggplant Chicken Wrap (see recipe page 137).

# VEAL POCKET NECK
## WITH PEAS & HASHU

### INGREDIENTS

veal pocket neck
salt
pepper
vegetable oil
water

Hashu balls (see recipe page 162)

2-3 medium size bags of frozen peas
2 tablespoons sugar
1-2 tablespoons Osem chicken consommé
1 teaspoon cinnamon
1 teaspoon allspice

1. Season the veal with salt and pepper. Coat the bottom of a wide pot with oil and heat the oil. Add veal to the pot and sear on both sides until nicely golden brown. Add water to cover ¼ of veal neck and transfer skillet to oven. Bake covered at 350°F for 1 hour.

2. Add Hashu balls, peas, salt, pepper, sugar, consommé, cinnamon and allspice around the veal. Return to oven and cook covered at 350°F for 2-2 ½ hours. (If water begins to dry out, add more hot water).

   Poke veal with a fork to ensure it is very tender before removing from oven. If not, cook for longer.

3. Serve veal in a large platter with Hashu balls and peas around it.

*These vegetable recipes are all simple and delicious, which can be used on their own or alongside any other dish!*

# JAPANESE VEGETABLE BOWL

### INGREDIENTS

2 pounds Skirt steak cut into strips or short ribs cut into thin slices (pepper steak can also be used)

**Alternate option:** 2 pounds chicken cutlets flat, cut into small strips

#### Steak or Chicken Sauce

½ cup soy sauce

¼ cup rice vinegar

¼ cup water

¼ cup chicken broth

2 tablespoons vegetable oil

1 tablespoon sesame oil

3 tablespoons brown sugar

1 teaspoon corn starch

½ teaspoon red pepper flakes

1 tablespoon sesame seeds

#### Brown Rice

2 cups brown rice

1 Vidalia onion, chopped

olive oil

4 cups of water

1 teaspoon Kosher salt

#### Carrots

10 carrots, cut in ¼'s (in half horizontally, then in half vertically)

2 tablespoons olive oil

1 ½ tablespoons agave

⅛ teaspoon cayenne pepper

3 tablespoons lime juice

1 tablespoon chopped fresh rosemary

#### Mushrooms

1 ½ pounds mixed mushrooms, i.e shitake maitake and oyster (bigger mushrooms should be cut into large chunks)

2 shallots, chopp'ed

1 Vidalia onion, chopped

olive oil

leaves of 1 sprig fresh rosemary, chopped

salt

pepper

6 slices Preserved Lemons (see recipe page 171), cut in ¼'s

#### Spinach

24 ounces fresh baby spinach

1 Vidalia onion, chopped

olive oil

½ teaspoon sesame oil

salt

pepper

cayenne pepper

1 teaspoon sesame seeds

#### Fried Egg (optional)

1 egg

Turn Page for recipe...

Now the recipe...

1. **Prepare steak or chicken:** Combine steak sauce ingredients and mix well. Place meat in a pot, top with steak sauce and bake covered at 350°F for 2 hours.

2. **Prepare brown rice:** Preheat oven to 350°F. Sautée onion in oil until its edges begin to golden. Add water and salt. When water boils, add brown rice. Boil for five minutes on the clock. Cover and transfer to oven for 1 hour.

   Prepare a wide skillet over the stove coated with 2 tablespoons olive oil. Transfer cooked rice to the skillet and cook on a low flame for 15-20 minutes Avoid mixing rice, allowing it to toast (yet being careful not to burn).

3. **Prepare carrots:** Place carrots on a greased baking tray and toss with oil, agave, cayenne pepper, lime juice and rosemary. Roast uncovered at 400°F for 45 minutes, turning once or twice in between.

4. **Prepare mushrooms:** Sautée shallots and onion together in oil until edges begin to golden.

   On a greased tray combine mushrooms, sautéed shallots and onions, rosemary, salt and pepper. Liberally oil mushrooms and mix well. Scatter preserved lemon quarters around mushrooms.

   Roast in oven uncovered at 400°F, for 40 minutes, tossing twice in between.

5. **Prepare spinach:** Sautée chopped onion in olive oil until its edges begin to golden. Add baby spinach, sesame oil, salt, pepper and cayenne pepper and cook until spinach just begins to wilt. Remove from heat
and add sesame seeds.

6. **Prepare fried egg (optional):** Coat the bottom of a small skillet with olive oil and allow oil to heat. Crack an egg and drop it directly into the pan. Allow egg to sit until the egg whites are set and the edges begin to curl up. Flip egg over and cook for one more minute.

7. **To serve:** Spoon crispy rice into the center of a large bowl. Neatly place carrots, mushrooms and spinach in sections around the rice. Lay cooked meat or chicken over the rice and top with 3-4 tablespoons of its juice, reserving the rest for individual use. Top meat with fried egg (if using) and serve.

*I like to give each of my guests a soup bowl for this dish so that they each take their favorite mixture of rice, meat/chicken and vegetables and enjoy all of the delicious flavors in one bowl!*

# CONDIMENTS

Preserved lemons......................................................171

Preserved Lemon Roasted Garlic Caesar Dressing.....173

Spicy Mayo............................................................175

Sweet Pesto...........................................................177

Lemony Pesto.........................................................177

Caramelized Onions................................................179

Oven Roasted Tomatoes..........................................181

Dill Mustard Sauce.................................................183

*I always have preserved lemons in my refrigerator and I add them to just about anything, from a tuna sandwich to chicken and potatoes and from any type of salad to any type of burger. It just adds a little kick and takes every dish to another level.*

# PRESERVED LEMONS

### INGREDIENTS

1 sterile ball jar
4-8 lemons, cut into thin rounds
1 tablespoon Kosher salt
1 tablespoon whole black peppercorns
2 bay leaves
¼ of a chili pepper, cut in ⅓'s (optional)
lemon juice
olive oil

1. Add 1 tablespoon kosher salt to bottom of mason jar. Begin stacking lemon rounds until jar is half way full. Add peppercorns, bay leaves and chili peppers (if using). Continue stacking remaining lemon rounds.

2. Fill the jar ¾ way with lemon juice, then add olive oil to fill the rest. Tightly seal jar and leave out 3-4 days, shaking it twice a day. Transfer to refrigerator and use with your favorite recipes.

   ** Lemon peel will soften after the first few days of refrigeration but can be used at any time.

   ** Preserved lemons can last for up to 4 weeks.

   ** Preserved Lemons are delicious when used with Stuffed Artichokes (see recipe page 66), Arugula Salad Pizza (see recipe page 90), Brussel Sprout Mozzarella Pizza (see recipe page 93), Quinoa with Roasted Mushrooms and Truffle oil (see recipe page 105), Tamarind Chicken (see recipe page 129), Tangy Meat Tacos (see recipe page 141), Preserved Lemon Caesar Dressing (see recipe page 173), and Lemony Pesto (see recipe page 177).

# PRESERVED LEMON ROASTED GARLIC CAESAR DRESSING

## INGREDIENTS

½ cup lemon juice

4 cloves of garlic, peeled then wrapped in aluminum and roasted in the oven at 350°F for 25 minutes

1 tablespoon dijon mustard

1 tablespoon red wine vinegar

1 cup olive oil

4 Preserved Lemons, (see recipe page 171)

3 anchovy fillets

Combine ingredients in a food processor and blend well.

\*\* Delicious when served with Warm Brussel Sprout Caesar Salad with homemade croutons (see recipe page 28) or any salad.

# SPICY MAYO

### INGREDIENTS

4 tablespoons mayonnaise
½ teaspoon sesame oil
½ teaspoon cayenne pepper
1 teaspoon Sriracha hot sauce

Combine ingredients and mix well.

** Spicy Mayo is delicious when served with Chicken Sliders (see recipe page 45), Crispy Rice (see recipe page 58), Blackened Grouper with Mango Corn Salsa (see recipe page 114) and Panko Crusted Tuna (see recipe page 116).

# SWEET PESTO

### INGREDIENTS

1 bunch fresh basil, cleaned and dried

1 handful yellow raisins

1 cup olive oil

salt

pepper

1 clove garlic

handful of pignoli nuts (optional)

grated Parmesan (optional)

Combine ingredients in a food processor and blend well. Add more oil if needed until desired consistency is reached.

** Pesto may be prepared in advance and frozen for later use.

** Pesto is delicious when served with Tofu Avocado Salad (see recipe page 20), Cheese Filled Wontons (see recipe page 51), Mediterranean Stuffed Tomatoes with Quinoa (see recipe page 55), Greek Portabella Pizzas (see recipe page 56), Eggplant Rollatini with Pesto (see recipe page 77), Arugula Salad Pizza (see recipe page 90) and Grilled Vegetable Pizza (see recipe page 94).

# LEMONY PESTO

### INGREDIENTS

1 bunch basil

2 slices Preserved Lemons, (see recipe page 171)

2 tablespoons Preserved Lemon juice, (see recipe page 171)

½ red chili pepper, seeds removed

2 cloves garlic

salt

pepper

1 cup olive oil

¼ cup pine or pistachio nuts, shelled (optional)

¼ cup parmesan cheese (optional)

Combine ingredients in a food processor and blend well. Add more oil if needed until desired consistency is reached.

** Pesto may be prepared in advance and frozen for later use.

** Lemony Pesto is delicious when served with Tofu Avocado Salad (see recipe page 20), Cheese Filled Wontons (see recipe page 51), Mediterranean Stuffed Tomatoes with Quinoa (see recipe page 55), Greek Portabella Pizzas (see recipe page 56), Arugula Salad Pizza (see recipe page 90) and Grilled Vegetable Pizza (see recipe page 94).

# CARAMELIZED ONIONS

### INGREDIENTS

2 Vidalia onions, cut into thin rounds
3 tablespoons olive oil
1 tablespoon balsamic vinegar

In a wide pan, combine onions and olive oil. Cook over the stove on a high fire for 25-30 minutes or until onions turn a golden brown color. Add balsamic vinegar and allow it to burn away for the last few minutes.

** Caramelized Onions can be prepared in advance and frozen for later use.

** Caramelized onions are delicious when served with **Chicken Sliders** (see recipe page 45), **Lamb Sliders** (see recipe page 45) and **French Cut Roast** (see recipe page 160).

# OVEN ROASTED TOMATOES

### INGREDIENTS

5 plum tomatoes, cut into ¼ inch thick rounds

salt

pepper

sugar

2 tablespoons chopped fresh basil

2 cloves garlic, crushed

olive oil

On a greased baking tray, lay tomatoes and sprinkle with salt, pepper, sugar, basil and garlic. Drizzle with olive oil and bake uncovered, at 300°F for 2 ½-3 hours.

\*\* Oven roasted tomatoes are delicious when served with Crispy Rice with Guacamole and Eggplant Miso (see recipe page 58) and Eggplant and Meatballs (see recipe page 147).

# DILL MUSTARD SAUCE

## INGREDIENTS

2 tablespoons honey mustard
1 tablespoon Dijon mustard
1 ½ tablespoon white wine vinegar
2 teaspoons sugar
salt
pepper
¼ cup oil
¼ cup chopped fresh dill

Combine all ingredients and mix well.

** Dill Mustard Sauce is delicious when served with Chicken Sliders (see recipe page 45), Grilled Salmon (see recipe page 119) and Tuna Burgers *(Dare to be Different, Dazzling dishes by Robin Jemal* see recipe page 103).